VALUE-BASED PARENTING

A Letter to Our Adult Children

Lee and JoAnne Bailey

Value Based Parenting © Copyright 2025 Lee and JoAnne Bailey

For more information, email baileybunch1993@gmail.com

ISBN: 979-8-89694-853-7 - Ebook

ISBN: 979-8-89694-854-4 - Paperback

DEDICATION

This book is dedicated to our parents, Charles, JoAnn, Joseph, and Jane, with much love and great appreciation. As our parents, you instilled values in us that have served us well. We are forever grateful to you for your sacrificial efforts in raising us, pouring into us, disciplining us, loving us, and encouraging us. This book would not exist without you.

And to our kids, Max, Levi, Emma, and Audrey, you bring us joy we can't express. The ability to live out through you all that is in this book has truly been the greatest of joys for us. It was difficult for sure, but the joys outweigh the sorrows by gallons. We pray that, as God gifts you with spouses and children, you will forge your own paths, make your own traditions, and hold fast to your values.

TABLE OF CONTENTS

Section 1

FIRST THINGS FIRST!

*"Your greatest contribution to the universe may
not be something you do, but someone you raise."*

—UNKNOWN AUTHOR

Max, Levi, Emma, and Audrey:

One day, as the story goes, a young child was watching her
mother carefully prepare Christmas dinner, and her mother did
something strange: She cut off both ends of the ham, about an
inch on either side, before placing it in the oven.

The little girl watched and wondered, and after thinking on it
for several minutes, she asked her mom why she did that. Her
mother paused and tilted her head slightly, eyes looking off
to the side as if she was thinking and searching for an answer.
She then turned to her daughter and simply said, "I don't
know. That's what my mom always did."

The mother decided to call her mom and ask about it. As
the two of them spoke on the phone while the child eagerly
listened, the grandmother, who had tried to come up with an

explanation and couldn't, just said, "You know, honey, I really don't know. That's what my mother always did."

Fortunately, her mother (the little girl's great-grandmother) was still living. Always delighted to hear from her daughter, she was so excited at the call. Now, three generations were curious about this practice of cutting off both ends of the Christmas ham.

The conversation quickly turned to laughter, however, when the ninety-two-year-old great-grandmother said, "Honey, my oven was too small for the ham; I had to cut the ends off to get it to fit."

This story is funny, but it also shows how easily we pass down routines without ever questioning them. Some traditions are beautiful and worth preserving. Others, if left unexplored, can become burdens we carry without understanding them. That's why we wrote this book: to explain the choices we made while raising you, so you won't just copy them blindly but actually know the "why" behind them.

The single purpose of this book is to avoid this dilemma. Good or bad, strong or weak, fast or slow, for whatever reason, in whatever state of mind we were in, we wanted to write down and explain why we did what we did as you all grew up.

We had our reasons. We tried our best, and we worked hard to be purposeful. We failed sometimes … miserably. But we had a few successes along the way, too.

Growing up in our home, you would have recognized that we did a few things differently.

We did that on purpose.

We set up a room without a TV so it would be centered on conversation.

We created an environment of questions, discussions, conversations, and debate. We insisted that all of you go to work at age fourteen. We kept you from smartphones and screens for as long as we could.

We created traditions we held fast to, such as family meals. We invited people over. We encouraged calculated risks. We sacrificed so you could have opportunities.

We homeschooled all of you from day one.

We didn't acknowledge Santa, the Easter Bunny, or the Tooth Fairy. We *never* let you sleep in our bed. We rarely took you to the doctor.

We asked you to classify your friends into color groups of red, yellow, and green.

We left you to cook and prepare your breakfast and lunch by and for yourselves by age twelve, and we taught you to take care of your laundry by that age, too.

You had chores that we *made* you do, and we didn't pay you to do them.

We made sure you had a place to volunteer your time.

We did not make you take standardized tests. We did not focus on grades.

Instead, we encouraged you to do your best, to give your all and have the right heart.

We expected you to give your best at every sports practice, every time you unloaded the dishwasher (you had to stack those Tupperware containers correctly!), and during every work shift.

We expected you to look adults in the eye and speak to them clearly and respectfully.

We focused on effort, not results. Winning a game or scoring a goal was not nearly as important as listening to your coach, playing your position correctly, and having the right attitude on the bench.

We taught you that there are winners and losers, and over your lifetime, winning will be based on your preparation, heart, grit, and determination. When you win, you'd better have earned it on the practice field, and when you lose, make a plan to prevent it from happening again.

We taught you that success in life is based largely on your ability to face rejection, defeat, and failure with open arms, as that is the best way to improve and grow.

We taught you that what you say about yourself *matters*, and we would not allow you to say things like "I'm not that good," or "I'll never get accepted," or "Life just isn't fair," or "I always spend all my money," and so on. Saying something out loud makes it truer and more permanent in your mind, and we wouldn't let you say such things.

When you stomped off and slammed the door, we made you come back, retrace your steps, and do it right this time. We made you repeat these steps until you could calmly walk to your bedroom and close the door quietly.

We taught you to say, "Yes, ma'am," and "Yes, sir."

We know, it probably felt weird at times. You may have thought we were the only parents on earth who did things this way. And honestly, we probably were. Over the years, other adults and even some family members questioned our decisions. They didn't understand why we made you work so young, why we didn't do Santa or why we didn't give you iPhones. But that didn't shake us. We knew what we were aiming for: confident, respectful, hardworking, grounded adults. Being different never bothered us, because we believed it would pay off in the long run.

Yes, we might have been considered different, harsh, even weird. But we had our reasons.

In fact, that is what this letter and this book are all about: our reasons.

Each one of you has graduated from high school and is on some level of a career path. But you haven't walked down the aisle yet, and you are not yet parents, so we thought this would be the perfect time to walk you through why we did what we did.

I heard Levi say recently, "Dad, I was going to come and ask your advice, but I already knew what you would say."

I suppose that's good. You heard from us so consistently that you have complete confidence in what we would say in most cases.

FROM MOM: You all know that your dad does a lot of the talking around the house, and this book is no different. He did a lot of the writing. You will hear his voice often as you read the words in this book. But at least once in every chapter, I want you to hear my voice. I want you to know you are reading the words your mamma wrote. While we are on the same page almost all of the time, sometimes I have a different perspective on things, and sometimes I outright disagree with your daddy. In those times, we have tried to show our different views. We love you bunches and hope you appreciate what we are trying to do with this book.

BUT DO YOU KNOW THE "WHY"?

What drove us to make some of the decisions we made? What happened to us? What made us the way we are that then drove us to create an intentional process to raise you and influence your thoughts and actions as best we could?

This isn't just a parenting book. It's a blueprint for reflection. We didn't write these chapters so you'd do everything exactly the same way we did. We wrote them so you wouldn't wake up one day and realize you're repeating habits and routines without knowing where they came from.

This was written to spell out our reasons. We wanted to leave you this book because one day you will be married, and one day you will have kids, and one day you will tell your kids about your childhood. And one day, we will no longer be here on earth.

We love you all dearly, and we already love your future spouses and future kids. We look forward to many years with all of you. But yes, one day, we will be gone. And it's with that in mind that we wrote this: to put to writing the reasons for everything we raised you to do and be.

Maybe you are a parent reading this book later on in your parenting journey, and perhaps you haven't parented "on purpose" in the ways this book lays out. Find comfort in knowing that God will bless your efforts even if you start late, but do not throw up your hands and give up. Children are resilient and smarter than we give them credit for, and given enough time, they will begin to live to a new standard (if the standard is expected consistently, of course). Serve the Lord faithfully, and raise your children as if it is your most sacred lifetime responsibility.

If your kids are older, you might even have them read portions of this book. We promise, children respond to consistent, loving discipline. They do not respond well to hateful, emotional scolding or humiliating verbal beatdowns. Begin with one concept and start setting a new standard within your home. It most certainly will be hard at first, but for their sake, facing a future in the real world where bosses and managers do not love them the way you do, it will be worth the effort.

> *"As a father shows compassion to his children, so the Lord shows compassion to those who fear Him." (Psalm 103:13)*

We labored through this book, editing, discussing, deleting, and rewriting, so that you would not cut off the ends of the Christmas ham just because we did.

Chapter 2

WHERE OUR VALUES COME FROM

*"In family life, love is the oil that eases
friction, the cement that binds closer together,
and the music that brings harmony."*

—Friedrich Nietzsche

One day, my brother and I (Dad) were throwing pillows at each other in the living room. Now, we had been instructed *not* to throw pillows, but as they say, boys will be boys. In all the excitement, a collectable Bugs Bunny glass, full of milk, was knocked over and broke!

My dad, the enforcer, was down the hall, and we knew he must have heard the noise. I immediately took my younger brother by the shoulders, looked him square in the eye, and said, "Okay, if Dad asks, this is what happened." I then made up the world's greatest, most impenetrable lie, a story that conveniently excluded the part where we were throwing pillows.

Sure enough, in mere minutes, our dad's shadow darkened the doorway. When he asked about the noise, I calmly told him about the "accident," how I had tripped and tragically knocked over the glass, but he needn't worry because I was already cleaning it up. My performance was extraordinary! My brother nodded along silently, like a good co-conspirator.

In that moment, we believed we had pulled off something heroic: We had created a version of the truth that protected us. This was our version of teamwork, even if it was completely dishonest.

A few minutes later, after the fear had left the room and we had celebrated our outrunning of justice, my dad, for reasons unknown, called my brother to his room. My mind had already drifted to my future life of crime when I suddenly heard my brother crying—uncontrollably, I might add.

The sound of those sobs changed everything. My celebration turned into dread. Even though I had convinced myself we'd fooled our dad, deep inside, I knew the truth would eventually surface.

When Dad called for me to join him in his room, I swallowed hard; I knew his interrogation techniques had broken my little brother. I was in for it now. My dad calmly explained that after only a few questions, my brother spilled the beans, so Dad spanked him with a homemade paddle for throwing pillows, as we had been told not to.

A homemade paddle may sound unusual today, but in many households at the time, it was a common disciplinary tool.

It was often kept in plain sight as a reminder. The message it carried was clear: Rules mattered, and disobedience had a cost.

I got the same corporal punishment. But after that misery was over, Dad took off his belt and explained that, while the paddling was for disobedience, this next punishment was for lying. That belt left a very clear impression, both on my backside and on my mind.

In our house, there was a difference between doing something wrong and lying to cover up wrongdoing. One could be corrected; the other broke trust. And once trust was broken, it had to be rebuilt slowly and carefully.

I feel the need to say this: I appreciate my dad for doing this. I was a very rambunctious kid, yet this is the only time I can remember him using this tactic. He reserved this type of correction for the times he wanted to make an impression. I do not have any feelings toward him other than love and respect. While this type of punishment might appear harsh, I can assure you that "a good talking-to" or some type of "grounding" would not have had the desired impact. I love my dad for making this point so vividly. This memory stayed with me not because of the pain but because of the principle. My dad believed there were moments in life when a lesson had to be unforgettable. Not every moment needed that weight, but this one did.

My dad valued honesty. No matter what, from that day forward, I sought to tell the truth. I recognized on that fateful pillow-throwing day that my parents hated lying more than any other shortcoming. This value became a guiding post for the rest of my life. I carried it into friendships, into marriage, into work. Honesty was not just about telling the truth. It was about being trustworthy, consistent, and whole.

As you read this book and try to understand why we wouldn't let you do this or that, why we emphasized certain things and seemed to disregard others, it will all come down to this: *values*.

Values are the silent engines that drive our decisions. You may not see them written on the wall, but they show up in every yes and no.

Whether people know it or not, their decisions are all based on their values. Those values may not be well-defined or easily articulated, but their decisions come from those values nonetheless.

Even people who say they are just "winging it" or "going with their gut" are still operating from a deeply held set of assumptions about what is good, right, or worthwhile. The difference is whether they have chosen those values on purpose or absorbed them by accident.

Here's an example: When a dad consistently—that is, not just once in a while but all the time—misses bedtime, ball games, school plays, and so on, whether he knows it or not, he values himself or his work above his family. Whether it comes from selfishness or exhaustion, this is a "me first" value. This man most likely says things like "What about me?" "I work hard to provide," "You never consider my feelings," "What I want doesn't matter," or "I have to think about myself sometimes."

The point is not to villainize parents who struggle with work-life balance. The point is to show how repeated choices paint a clear picture. Even when their words say one thing, actions reveal a person's true priorities.

A more positive example is someone who chooses to buy food at the grocery store and cook meals at home. This person values the responsible management of money; they are willing to be temporarily inconvenienced with cooking and cleaning instead of spending significantly more money going out to eat.

This example seems small, but it carries real weight. Our values often show up in our quiet, repetitive choices. They shape not just how we spend our money, but how we spend our days.

So, where do your values come from? Where did your parents' (your mom's and my) values come from?

We love this quote from Corrie ten Boom, who helped hide Jews during the Holocaust and was eventually imprisoned in a concentration camp for those actions:

> *"Every experience God gives us, every person He puts in our lives is the perfect preparation for the future that only He can see."*

This quote captures a deep belief we hold: Our values are not formed in isolation. They are shaped through people, moments, trials, and routines. They grow slowly over time, like roots that run deep before the branches ever emerge.

OUR PARENTS

This goes without saying, but much of what we believe and value comes from the households we grew up in. Fortunately for us (and for you), we didn't have to deal with competing values from different sets of parents, since all your grandparents held similar values.

That kind of alignment is rarer than it seems. Many couples spend years trying to reconcile the ways they were raised. I have done hundreds of hours of premarital counseling, and I can tell you that, without question, many couples go into marriage with a stated goal of "not doing what their parents did." In our case, our shared values gave us a strong foundation and fewer surprises. They also gave us a model of what unity in parenting could look like.

> **WARNING:** *This is our first warning to you. When you date and eventually marry, your partner's family's values will matter to you; they will either be a help to your marriage or a real issue. Things that you might never expect to be problems can be, and those problems can cause other problems, until all of a sudden, you and your future spouse are straight up mad at each other because you can't agree on how to handle your money, how to raise your kids, or where to go to church. Much of this—not all of it, but much of it—comes from the*

*way you were raised. If you find someone who was raised radically different from you, your values may never align. Be careful. This may not seem urgent in your current stage of life, but it is one of the most important truths we can share with you. Marriage is about more than love or attraction; it is about shared direction. And **direction is set by values.***

Your mom and I feel incredibly blessed to have been raised by parents who love each other, who work hard, and who care deeply for others. These are hints at the values we will talk about in the rest of this book. When you see us prioritize relationships, put effort into hard work, or give someone our attention, it is not random. It is rooted in how we were raised. We hope to pass those habits and instincts down to you.

FROM DAD: To be raised by your grandmommy and granddaddy was an incredible blessing. We laughed a lot. We ate around the dinner table. We had tons of discussions about everything. They, of course, loved their parents, and I saw how they took care of them and spent time with them. I used to love when my grandfather (Ralph Bailey), Granddaddy's father, would call the house phone; my dad would answer and then immediately get comfortable. Ralph would talk on and on and on, and my dad would often fall asleep listening to him. But not once did I ever hear him talk back, cut him off, or be disrespectful in any way. Respect was modeled for me, so I learned to respect my parents, even when they weren't around. Respect was not demanded in our home; it was lived out. Watching my dad honor his father taught me more than any lecture could have. It showed me that respect is a way of being, not a rule to be followed.

Grandmommy was a stay-at-home mom, and she always had dinner ready at 5:00 p.m. We never went out to eat. Grandaddy was a pastor at a local Baptist church, and that church didn't have a great place for an office, so he kept an office at home. When I tell you that having access to both my parents during the day was a special blessing, I mean it. If I had a question for Mom, she was always nearby to answer. Whether I had a deep spiritual question or I wanted clarification on the infield fly rule in baseball, I could gently knock on Dad's office door, and he would welcome me in and answer me without making me feel like I was bothering him. They were present. That is what I remember most. Not extravagant vacations or big-ticket items, but consistent availability. I never had to wonder if my parents would be there. And that stability created deep security.

We played outside all the time. We didn't have access to video games or cable TV, so instead, we wrestled or rode our bikes. We lived on forty acres of land, so climbing trees and digging in the dirt were common activities as well.

We went to church, of course, every Sunday morning, Sunday night, and Wednesday night, as well as any other night the church had activities or revivals or Vacation Bible School.

Faith was not a separate compartment. It was integrated into the rhythm of our lives. Church was not just a Sunday obligation but part of the culture we lived in daily.

FROM MOM: Growing up in Mamaw and Papaw's house was a little different than your dad's experience. Since both of them were school teachers, we were out the door pretty early every morning. While Mom was getting ready, Dad made us breakfast almost every morning. We especially loved it when he made blueberry pancakes, made from blueberries that we as a family would go pick in late summer every year.

When Mom came home from teaching school, we would start prepping supper. We always ate around the table. Mom would have us make certain dishes, side dishes, or desserts, and that is how I learned to cook. Cooking together was a way to pass down recipes, but also a time to talk, to learn patience, and to contribute to the good of the group. That kind of daily collaboration builds a mindset of service and teamwork.

I loved sitting on my dad's lap and reading the comics from the Sunday morning newspaper. We always had ice cream in the freezer, and we would always gather on Sunday evenings to watch the movie of the week on *The Wonderful World of Disney*. We loved the holidays, and I particularly loved traveling down to Mississippi to visit my grandmother. Those small joys created warmth in our home. Traditions, even simple ones, help create family identity. They give kids a sense of belonging that lasts far beyond childhood.

I liked going to church with my parents; we always attended, just like your dad, every time the doors were opened. I enjoyed the missions part of our Wednesday night activities, and I loved Sunday school. We were always involved in everything. And we loved it. Involvement was not seen as a burden; it was expected and embraced. That regular rhythm of participation helped shape my view that community and commitment go hand in hand.

Because my sister (your aunt) was a full five years older than me, I feel like she was often the third parent in the house. When Mom and Dad weren't around, I knew I could count on DeAnne to be there to help me with stuff, play with me, and make me feel safe when I crawled into bed with her at night. Siblings can shape values just as much as parents. That early sense of security and closeness built a foundation of trust that still matters today.

So many of our collective values came from the people who raised us. Beyond our parents, our aunts, uncles, grandparents, and parents' friends all had a part in shaping our value system. We learned *a lot* from just being around our parents and seeing them interact with their friends. We saw them care for each other, laugh and cry with each other. We saw them handle difficult situations with class and difficult people with dignity.

Children are always watching. They learn more from how we live than from what we say. The examples we saw were not perfect, but they were sincere. And they stayed with us.

OUR GRANDPARENTS/OTHER FAMILY MEMBERS

FROM DAD: It wasn't just our parents who shaped our values; our grandparents did, too. I suffered a tragedy when I was only four years old: My biological mother (Jane Davenport Bailey) passed away unexpectedly of spinal meningitis. While this had a profound impact on me and my brother, it gave us something that few people in this world get: a third set of grandparents. After Mom died, Dad eventually remarried, and Grandmommy's parents became our third complete set of grandparents. This unexpected extension of our family added more than just people to our holiday dinners. It gave us more models of marriage, more stories about sacrifice, and more love. Each set of grandparents had slightly different personalities, but their values echoed each other. That consistency made it easier for us to absorb those values as part of who we were becoming.

I was incredibly lucky. All three sets of grandparents had similar values, worked hard, loved us unconditionally, and were good people who loved their spouses. We got to see our grandfathers showing love to our grandmothers and our grandmas taking care of our grandads. They never competed for attention among themselves, but they were always available and caring, and I learned a great deal about life from all six of them. Much of my value system was shaped by them.

When our mom passed, your Uncle Jackson and I moved into our aunt's house for a while. Aunt Piney and Uncle D, as they were affectionately nicknamed, took us in while we recovered from Mom's death. Living with someone, especially when you are under the age of five, will have an impact and certainly play a role in the development of your values. We were blessed to have aunts and uncles who spoke into our lives, too. At that age, you do not have the words to express grief, confusion, or gratitude. You just feel it. You feel the care, the consistency, and the presence of people who are there for you. And that leaves a lasting impression.

Of course, Jackson and I both look at Aunt Piney (our mom's older sister) and Uncle D as a pair of surrogate parents for a season in our very impressionable years. The houseful of cousins didn't hurt, either. We felt loved and taken care of during a time when my dad (your grandad) was clearly grieving. Even in sorrow, our family taught us how to be steady. We watched adults carry burdens and still show up for the next generation. That taught us strength without words.

FROM MOM: I had a different experience from your dad. Grandmother (Papaw's mom) was the only grandparent I ever knew. But she had the presence of all four; we spent so much time together when I was young, I don't feel like I missed out at all. While my mom helped shape my overall love for cooking, family, and togetherness, my grandmother reinforced those values over and over again. Togetherness, cooking and baking, playing games and cards, going to work with her— these things helped to shape my thoughts and values. Although I didn't have as many grandparents as your dad, the beauty of this relationship was in its depth. The one-on-one time I had with my grandmother made a lasting impression on me that I cannot adequately express with words.

My mom has a twin sister (Aunt Jean), and we often visited with her and Uncle Ellis. They loved and cared for us, and they helped reinforce my parents' values. So, also, did Uncle Bill. He was so sweet and fun to be with when we were growing up, but it wasn't until he married Aunt Sherry (the same year your daddy and I married) that we got to see the real Uncle Bill. We love and appreciate all of our aunts, uncles, and cousins and the way they helped shape our thoughts, values, and attitudes.

TELEVISION

Neither of us is proud to admit this, but growing up, TV influenced both of us in who we became and how we later raised you.

When it came to values, the networks and their commentators seemed to stay out of anything other than the sport they were commenting on. Rarely was I exposed to editorials by my favorite broadcasters. Instead, I saw interviews with the athletes, and they always thanked God, thanked their coaches, and attributed their success to their hard work in the off-season. That reinforced what we were taught at home.

WARNING: *This is our second warning for you as future parents. TV was so much more family-friendly when we were young and impressionable. Now, kids don't even watch network TV anymore. They watch videos on TikTok and YouTube (and who knows what else by the time you have kids of your own). These are not nearly as regulated as network TV was in the '80s. So as parents, you'll not only have to worry about what your kids watch, but when. Screens used to be in the middle of our living room. They were never in our laps to look at any time, day or night. This makes it all the more important that you instill the right values* *in your kids. When everything is instant, influence is constant. Decide what you will allow to take root.*

FROM DAD: Television for me was comedies and sports. We never had cable TV, so we only watched the three main networks using an antenna on our roof. I craved sports on television, so I watched whatever the networks would show, from Saturday morning tennis to Monday Night Football! I loved it when a Reds or Braves baseball game was on during the week, which was very, very rare. The only sports I regularly got to watch were playoffs that were shown during prime time. This is why I *loved* the Olympics and Bowl games so much: They gave me an opportunity to watch sports day and night for several weeks in a row.

Outside of sports, sitcoms ruled my TV life. *The Andy Griffith Show, Happy Days, Lavern and Shirley, Family Ties, Who's the Boss, The Cosby Show, Cheers*, and *Home Improvement* were the mainstays of my childhood. All those shows also reinforced what I was taught at home: Show respect to everyone (especially your parents), do the right thing, and love each other. Even the show set in a Boston bar had a very family-centric feel to it. (Sure, it was a dysfunctional group, but lightheartedly so.)

FROM MOM: We watched a lot of game shows. We always watched *Wheel of Fortune* and *Jeopardy* right after dinner. I liked the sitcoms that were on during my childhood, like *The Cosby Show, Cheers, Family Ties, Silver Spoon, Facts of Life*, and *Growing Pains*. All of these shows, in one way or another, reinforced our views of family, togetherness, honesty, and friendships. None of the shows I watched were in direct opposition to what my parents taught us.

FRIENDS

Among the people who helped shape our thoughts, values, and actions were the friends we had. We both had some good friends and some bad friends. Like many people, I (Dad) was intrigued by the people who were arrogant and troublemakers. In middle school, I hung out with some of those kids, and I learned a lot of terrible things from them. I was so naive that I didn't understand what I was saying; I just thought it was cool. This phase is not unusual. Children often mimic what they hear, especially when it earns a laugh or gives them a sense of belonging. At that age, we want to fit in more than we want to be wise. But those early influences, even the harmful ones, taught me important lessons about the power of words and the cost of following the crowd.

I remember one time, I came home and told my dad a very crude joke. To his credit, he realized I didn't have an earthly idea what any of it meant, and he was gracious about pointing out my ignorance.

In middle school, everybody played some kind of sport, so I also found both good and bad influences among my teammates. Fortunately, when the action got a little more advanced, most of those I would consider a negative influence would drop out of the sport or get in so much trouble that it wasn't worth staying. This is when the quality of my friends took a big step forward. I started hanging out with others who cared a lot about athletics and sports. Our families also seemed to share similar values: hard work, discipline, respect, resilience, and sportsmanship.

FROM MOM: I played with friends who lived nearby, and at least one of them is still a good friend of mine to this day. I didn't have many friends who took me down a path wildly different from my upbringing. What was *really* different in our house was the fact that we seemed to always have someone staying with us. We had numerous foreign exchange students: at least two students from Japan, as well as students from Denmark and Norway. I grew up in a home where we brought different cultures—but not necessarily different values—into our home. That kind of exposure made a lasting difference. I learned to see people through the lens of their shared humanity, not just their backgrounds. It showed me that people from around the world can value kindness, family, honesty, and hard work just as much as we do.

One of my fondest experiences was an unlikely friendship I formed with a girl from England. Her name was Emma Scarboro. (Does that first name sound familiar?) In fourth grade, our teacher asked us who wanted to be the pen pal (that's what they called someone who exchanged letters with people in other cities or countries) of someone from England. I volunteered, and we began a habit of writing letters to each other that lasted for years. It culminated in me visiting her and staying with her family in England. We visited all the wonderful places in England, and I remember their family being surprisingly similar to ours.

THE BIBLE

For anyone growing up in a Christian home, the Bible should be the source of all the values they hold dear. That is not the case with everyone, of course. Some so-called Christian families never reference Scripture, never quote from it, and never use its principles to explain why a certain decision was or was not made. There are also families who do not claim to be Christian, but whose upbringing nevertheless leads them to raise their families with biblical values.

In both of our homes, we were taught Scripture from a very early age as the basis of all our decisions. In fact, we both believe that the majority of the values we were raised under were taken from the Bible. Scripture was not used to control or shame, but to explain. When our parents said no, they often followed it up with a biblical principle that made sense. Over time, that helped us internalize those values instead of just obeying them temporarily.

What we find sad is that many, many families make decisions based on emotions, and those decisions are often not tied to a sound value. Any decision could be different based on the way a parent feels at a given moment. This creates confusion for kids. Inconsistent correction sends the message that rules are about moods, not meaning. On the other hand, when decisions come from anchored values, kids are more likely to understand and respect them, even if they disagree.

When it came to the values that our parents, our grandparents, our friends, and even television in the '80s seemed to point to, the Bible was the common denominator.

> **WARNING:** *Here's our third warning to you as future parents. God's Holy Word is being dismissed and pushed aside more and more each passing year. You will not have the luxury of having all your kids' friends and their entertainment choices reinforce your own parental values. You must be careful and diligent (not helicopter parents, but not lazy, either) to stay in close touch with your kids, their friends, and what they all watch and listen to. We are not saying they should never be exposed to values that do not align with yours. In fact, that is probably healthy. But when your kids are being* **influenced** *by values outside of what you hold dear, you need to ask yourselves important questions: "Why? Am I not living out my own values? Do my kids not see the reason why we do what we do? Am I being a lazy parent by not spot-checking them? Am I creating a household environment in which their friends* **don't** *want to come to our house? Is my teaching and correcting consistent enough for my kids to even know what my values are?"*

Where do your values come from?

The rest of this book will seek to spell out our own values and how those values shaped our decisions. We wrote this in love. Remember, you are loved, and we already love your future spouses and future children. We are praying for those spouses and kids often, and we look forward to meeting them!

In the meantime, we wanted to write down all the things that you might ask as you begin your own journey. This book is for each of you and your future families. Think of this not as a rulebook but as a trail of breadcrumbs. These are the things we hope you will remember when you are unsure, when you are building your own families, and when you are struggling to choose between what is easy and what is right.

For anyone outside our family reading this, we encourage you—beg you, even—to seek to understand what your values are and to live by them. Do not leave this to chance. A life without clear values will always be pulled in a hundred directions. But a life anchored in purpose and principle, even when it is hard, leads to peace.

YOUR VALUES CHECKLIST

- Have you given any thought to where your values come from?

- Can you identify your own personal values in a clear and concise manner?

- Do you have values that may have controlled your decisions in the past and that you need to replace with a different set of values?

- Be careful how much you allow social media, television, Google, and AI to shape who you are.

- You are unique; do not allow "the crowd" to make your decisions for you.

Chapter 3

BEGIN WITH THE END IN MIND

*"All the gold which is under or upon the earth
is not enough to give in exchange for virtue."*

—Plato

RAISING ADULTS STARTS WHEN YOU BRING THEM HOME

Is it ever "too late" to truly begin parenting? If you have been slacking in your parenting responsibilities, and now your kids are ten, twelve, or even fifteen, is it too late to begin to instill values that you didn't instill when they were young? I guess it depends. Our advice is to never give up. But it is possible to start so late that they don't have time to internalize those values before they move out.

The key here is not to let guilt over the past paralyze you. Begin where you are, with what you know now. Values are caught more than taught, and your consistency moving forward can still impact your kids, even if the foundation wasn't solid from the start.

Remember, children—at any age—are always watching.

On the other hand, is there an age that is too young to begin teaching? To this question, we both believe the answer is a resounding "No!"

Infants learn patterns and expectations almost immediately. Their brains are designed to make sense of the world around them, even before they can speak or crawl. That's why the earliest months matter, because they are forming connections and responses to your leadership from day one.

As we got ready to bring Max home, we were so pleased to have read and reread the book *On Becoming Babywise* by Gary and Anne Marie Ezzo. As of writing this, we know that the Ezzos faced numerous battles that challenged their teachings, and we also understand that not everyone embraces the philosophy espoused in their books. However, when you are very young and very insecure about your parenting, reading a book like that and implementing a plan gives you a certain amount of confidence.

This was the beginning of us doing things "with purpose." With the tremendous help of our dear friends, Joel and Wendy Benson, we began the purposeful and deliberate plan to put Max (and eventually his siblings who came along after him) on a routine, and decided early on that putting our kids in our bed was not something we were going to do.

Even though Max was especially fragile when he came home, we felt strongly that from day one, he would need to be able to settle himself down and not rely on us to get to sleep. Anyone reading this might think this seems cold and heartless, but trust us, it was the exact opposite.

We knew that sleep training, boundaries, and consistency would eventually lead to a more secure child and a more peaceful home. In the short term, it felt difficult, especially when the world said to respond to every cry. But our decision was rooted in love, not detachment.

We believed it was important to begin early to teach a few things from the start: First, we were in control, not the baby we'd just brought home. Second, even in Max's infant stages, we needed to prioritize our marriage. Third, we believed that all children are a blessing and that God gave Max (and all our future children) to *us* to raise, so we would make that—the raising of children—one of our top adult jobs.

That job requires intention. Raising children is more than feeding and changing diapers. It's forming a worldview. Every decision in those early months either supports or undermines the ideas of who's in charge, what matters most, and how the child fits into the bigger picture of a healthy home.

In the chapters that follow, we will lay out each individual *value* that we hold dear as parents, so you can see why we did what we did. In this chapter, however, we want to explain a few things about the infant/newborn situation before you have kids of your own.

FROM MOM: When you have babies (my grandbabies!), I am going to try so hard to stay out of your business. You see, we worked and worked and worked on learning how to help newborns sleep through the night, how to keep them on a schedule that puts the parents in control, and how to still get sleep even when you have an infant. So if your dad and I see or hear you complaining about "sleepless nights" or "getting our days and nights turned around," trust me, it will be an act of incredible restraint to not jump in. We did that experiment on all four of you. We did the hard work, and we truly want to be a source of experience for you so you don't have to endure what most first-time parents go through.

BABY SIGNS

We also wanted to include here the value we placed on baby sign language. We came to understand early in parenting that kids understand well before they can talk. So we read up on and instituted the art and science of sign language to help you talk to us before you could form words. Let me tell you (and anyone else reading this), if you think this whole idea is crazy, we thought the same thing—until we tried it ourselves.

We weren't language development experts. We were just trying to get through the day without a meltdown. But baby signing became a surprising win. It helped bridge that frustrating gap between understanding and expression, and it gave us peace in moments that could have turned chaotic.

We spent so many months early on teaching you how to use your hands for words and phrases like "food," "drink," "thank you," "all done," and "book." Simple, easy hand motions replaced the grunting and screaming that kids normally do when they can't talk yet.

If you think this is nuts, consider how easy it is to teach a six-month-old child how to wave goodbye. Signing is the same thing. Communication is only limited by your own imagination and consistency in teaching them each hand gesture.

We found we were a little sad when the signing stopped. It was a sweet way for you to communicate, but once you started talking, the signing ceased almost overnight.

WHO'S IN CHARGE, ANYWAY?

Indeed, the question we asked ourselves the most when we had newborns was this: "Who is in charge?" The point was to remind us that God gave us (the parents) thinking minds, judgment, experience, common sense, family, friends, the Bible, and other resources, while the baby just has a crying reflex for everything. Why then would we allow the newborn to control everything we did for the next two years? Why would we let Max, crying at 2:00 a.m., keep us from going back to bed after he was fed and had his diaper changed? Could we, in good conscience and in a healthy way, coax and train this little fella to adhere to our schedule?

This wasn't about dominating our children. It was about stewarding them. We were not afraid to take the lead because we believed God had given us that responsibility.

So, with the help of friends and a few good books, we embraced the idea that God is not the Creator of chaos, but the Author of order. We also adopted the belief that, while we were imperfect and very mistake-prone, of the three of us, Mom and I were the two smartest people in the house.

We kept Max (and all his siblings) from eating until the appointed time. We made sure he ate a complete meal, not just a little snack because he was sleepy/hungry or had a wet diaper. We kept him awake with all our might until his appointed bedtime. All of this put him on a predictable eat/wake/sleep schedule within two weeks of being home from the hospital, and by the nine-week mark, he was sleeping through the night (six to seven hours) and never reverted. We repeated this with Levi, Emma, and Audrey, all with the same results.

Even at this early stage of parenting, we began to understand that having a purpose in mind—an end goal—helps with the day-to-day difficulties of parenting. Consistency, not perfection, was the target. And the fact that we knew what was best for our kids was our first parenting value.

WE LEARNED FROM OTHERS' MISTAKES

Fortunately for us, we had lots of friends who had babies before we did, so we had already heard all the horror stories of bedtime with an infant. Many of our friends told us that they had brought a crying baby to their bed "just this one time"—and their three-year-old was still sleeping with them all the time. I don't know about you, but having another human (or even a dog) in your bed would hamper your spontaneity substantially.

Our friends would tell us how this arrangement impacted the intimate nature of their relationship and how it ruined their sleep for years because (1) they were terrified of rolling over on the baby, so they never quite went to sleep; and (2) their little toddler had gotten so used to it that they did not know how to get the child back in their own bed. Knowing what a huge problem it was, we made the difficult choice early on to *never* let our kids sleep with us.

This decision wasn't based on fear or distance. It was based on wisdom we had gained from the honest regrets of people we loved. They didn't mean to drift away from their marriages. But inch by inch, sacrifice by sacrifice, they slowly placed the marriage second, then last. We weren't willing to make that trade.

I don't know if our original intent was to prioritize our marriage, but that soon became the main reason behind our decision. We saw through our friends and acquaintances that when a child becomes the primary person in the household, things get messed up pretty fast. Usually, Dad becomes nothing more than an errand boy as Mom is ordered around by the four-year-old who's in charge of the whole house. We witnessed this before we were parents ourselves, and we noticed it usually happened to the parents who started off putting their crying child on a pedestal and catering to their every whim, naturally causing their marriage to fracture.

Having been parents now for over twenty-five years, we've noticed that very few of our divorced friends, peers, and acquaintances split before kids. Most got divorced some years after they started having kids, and when asked why, they said, "We just drifted apart." That phrase, "drifted apart," sounds passive, like a tide pulling people away from shore. But it's not; it's hundreds of small, daily choices to stop pursuing, stop prioritizing, stop checking in, until eventually, the person across the dinner table becomes a stranger.

> **WARNING**: *Kids, if you ever think that you and your spouse are "drifting apart," **do not** ignore the thought. **Do not** assume it will fix itself. **Do not** assume that your spouse will come to the same conclusion and bring it up. This is too important to ignore. The moment, the millisecond, you begin to think that some magic is eroding, deal with it. Marriage is so hard to keep fresh for years and years. There will be times when it is fresher than others. There will be times when you are clicking and other times when you are not. That is the natural flow of life. But **do not** allow too much time to go by before you address it. A small, uncomfortable conversation now is worlds better than the conversation that you want to go to marriage counseling. A good, Christian, Bible-based marriage counselor can be a marriage-saver, but we would still prefer you do what you can to avoid being in that position to begin with. Oh, and never use the word "divorce." It's a terrible word that is often used as a weapon during a fight. Refrain from that. You are better than that.*

So, as a strongly held value, we knew we had to prioritize our marriage. Of course, that did not mean that we loved you any less than anyone else loves their children. It's just that we intentionally put you in second place to our own relationship. That may sound countercultural, but it's biblical. Genesis 2:24 reminds us that a man leaves his father and mother and holds fast to his wife, and the two become one flesh. That oneness is not optional; it's foundational.

We will say—and this is not based on science but on our own experience—we believe this next statement as strongly as we believe any truth:

The best predictor of a child's success as a productive member of society is that they grew up in a home in which their mom and dad genuinely loved each other.

OUR CHILDREN, THE ARROWS

In Genesis 1, we read about the entire creation story: what happened on day one, day two, and so forth. At the end of each day, the Bible records that God looked around, observed what He had made on that particular day, and said to Himself, "This is good!"

Then, the Bible records God looking over the finished product at the end of day six. Considering it and observing His creation, He said to Himself, "This is *very good!*"

It is our belief that God would *not* have said that if He intended for children to be the element that completes a family. At that time, God had made both Adam and Eve, but no children had been born, so God was saying that a world with just husband and wife is a complete and "good" thing. So, we firmly hold to the truth that no marriage is incomplete without kids.

> **WARNING:** *To our wonderful children, we will terrorize you and toilet paper your yard if you so much as consider using the phrase "start a family" when referring to having children. The day you walk down the aisle is the day you start a family, and it is already complete in God's eyes. Children are a welcome addition to an already established family. It's okay; if you forget, we will gladly remind you!*

Yes, the psalmist writes in Psalm 127:3–4:

> *Behold, children are a heritage from the Lord,*
> *the fruit of the womb a reward.*
> *Like arrows in the hand of a warrior*
> *are the children of one's youth.*

So, we do believe that children are a blessing. In fact (as you'll understand in Chapter 4), Mom and I used to discuss at home what to say to strangers who would stop us at one of our frequent grocery store runs, after we had our third and fourth child, and say things like "Wow, you have your hands full!" or "You do know what causes that, don't you?"

We took our line of thinking from that Psalm passage. Every time a slightly negative or even neutral comment was made, we would say, "They are such a blessing!"

We repeated that often. Yes, parenting newborns, toddlers, and stinky little elementary-aged boys is challenging, but it is also a true blessing and a privilege.

We accidentally read a book (more on that later) written by Vickie Farris. The title, *A Mom Just Like You*, was intriguing because of the size of her family (ten kids) and the fact that she homeschooled. We had been toying with the idea of homeschooling and were going over the pros and cons when this book came across our path. Because this mom suggested she was just like any other mom and she was homeschooling all ten of her kids, we decided to read it.

This is the "accidental" part: Vickie Farris lays out in the book how she and her husband arrived at the idea that God did not want them to prevent pregnancy artificially, so they wound up with ten kids. Her research and reasoning were quite compelling: Nowhere in Scripture does it say to prevent or limit family size, nor is there anything about children *other than* them being a blessing. Her reasoning was "Why would we intentionally prevent a blessing out of convenience or some contrived notion of financial preservation?"

After reading that, your mom and I were convinced. After we had Max, we stopped preventing. Yep, we had tons and tons of unprotected sex! We embraced the idea that children were a blessing and we should allow God to bless us as much as possible. After Mom stopped nursing Max, we got pregnant with Levi. The same cycle held true through each pregnancy, to the point where we calculated Mom was pregnant or nursing for around 95 out of 100 months during the early 2000s.

We were gathered together in the operating room during Emma's C-section (Mom had all four of you via C-section) when we heard the doctor say, "Oh no!" Not a comforting sound for me, coming from the man who'd just opened up my wife. He was a slow-speaking doctor, and it felt like minutes before he gathered himself enough to explain.

He told us the uterus was not growing uniformly and that it was extremely dangerous to continue to have children, as a rupture during a future pregnancy was highly likely. A rupture while pregnant would endanger both the mom and the baby, so he told us to stop at three. I don't know if it was my utter spiritual stubbornness, the fun of unprotected sex, or the fact that I was terrified of a vasectomy, but we didn't stop at three. We believed that God wanted us to keep having kids because we truly believed—we had a stated value, you could say—that children are a blessing.

We finally chose to stop after four, but it wasn't easy. It felt like we were going back on a promise. But sometimes obedience means adjusting when new wisdom or information is revealed. We didn't stop believing children were a blessing. We just recognized the limits of our own health and circumstances.

After the fourth pregnancy, the doctor made us so afraid we were living dangerously that we reluctantly made some medical decisions to prevent all future pregnancies. While Mom was open deep and wide again for a fourth C-section, they would "tie her tubes." I was able to snake my way out of a vasectomy after all.

We felt a little like hypocrites after we made that decision. We had marched to the beat of the drum that said, "You shouldn't artificially limit family size," and yet we did. Eventually, we got past that feeling, but writing about it here has brought those feelings back.

You see, we made the slightly immature decision to "preach" the idea of family size to others. With almost too much pomp, we would tell people we were okay with whatever number of children God might bless us with. We often talked about having ten or more. But the truth is that it scared us. Ten children would be extremely hard to handle, but we were too proud to admit that. We dutifully went about our business of having more kids, until our doctors told us not to. It was then that we faced our own fear. We backed down from a stance that was not even clear-cut in Scripture. It was only an interpretation of Scripture from someone we had never met.

There's freedom in admitting your faults, in learning and adjusting, in surrendering pride while still honoring conviction. God never called us to fake consistency. He called us to walk in wisdom.

It was a healthy friction, the friction between marriage and parenting, that helped shape us. Marriage was our top priority, but children are a blessing—those two ideals molded our philosophy from beyond the newborn stages. We knew we needed to be there for our kids, show them that we love them, and demonstrate consistency in their discipline, instruction, and growth, while *at the same time* investing in our marriage, continuing to date, and having fun as a couple. And somehow, we had to do all of that while paying bills and living life.

How do you shape and mold your life around the responsibility of raising warriors, around the idea that your kids are arrows for good in the world, while also preserving the sweet freshness of a loving marriage?

These decisions, these actions, these discussions became part of who we are and who we will always be. We became passionate about marriage quality and just as passionate and intentional about parenting.

A strong partnership in marriage is vital to pulling this off. Both of you must be on the same page and willing to forgive each other in moments of failure, as there surely will be.

The following chapters will lay out what we learned along the way and what we want to pass on to you. It is our best effort to help you learn from *our* mistakes, so you at least don't have to repeat them while you make mistakes of your own.

FROM MOM: As your dad has stated, we struggled with balance. We struggled with maintaining a schedule. But we never quit. We never stopped trying. If you are blessed with children, let us help you, even if it's only to babysit now and then so you and your spouses can have date nights.

PRIORITIES CHECKLIST

- As future parents, what are your priorities?
- As future parents, who is your priority?
- Do you have a parenting philosophy?
- Do not allow "life" to get in the way of your marriage. You *can* have a great marriage and focus on your children at the same time!

Section 2

VALUES

The Value of Purpose

The Value of Respect

The Value of Diligence

The Value of Self-Discipline

The Value of Humility

The Value of Being a Lifetime Learner

The Value of Generosity

The Value of Marriage

The Value of Faith

The Value of Righteousness

The Value of Words

The Value of Love

The Value of Thinking for Yourself

The Value of Traditions

The Value of Hospitality

The Value of Purity

Chapter 4

THE LIVING ROOM VS. THE GROCERY STORE

"There is one quality which one must possess to win, and that is definiteness of purpose, the knowledge of what one wants, and a burning desire to possess it."

—NAPOLEON HILL

THE VALUE OF PURPOSE

Have you ever witnessed a four-year-old having a meltdown in the middle of a department store?

Have you ever watched a seven-year-old beg and beg for candy at the checkout line?

Have you ever seen a twelve-year-old being disrespectful to a fast-food worker or a waitress?

Have you ever heard a child make a borderline racist comment while standing in line at the post office?

Well, our answer to all of those questions is yes—and they were all our own kids!

Parenting, in its rawest form, is humbling. You think you're teaching, but so often, you're being taught. We've been on the receiving end of glares from strangers. And what we've realized over time is that those moments are not proof of failure, but invitations to lead better, teach deeper, and listen closer.

What do you do when your kids act up or do something that embarrasses you in public?

The values we wanted to teach you, the ones we believed mattered most, needed the right environment. Some places make learning almost impossible, especially when emotions are high or the setting is full of distractions. Trying to teach in the middle of a tantrum at the store often does more harm than good. That's why we chose to teach the most important lessons in a place where you could really listen, reflect, and grow: the living room.

THE LIVING ROOM

Your mom and I both agree that the single best *practical* parenting decision we made was to create a room in our house void of distraction. In every home we lived in, the living room was our conversation room.

I remember reading the daily comics as a kid, and I was a big fan of *The Far Side* by Gary Larson. I have never forgotten how ridiculous a certain one of those single-panel comics looked to me: An entire family was gathered around facing a blank wall. They were arranged in a perfect semicircle in a stereotypical middle-class home. There was a dad in a comfy armchair, and on the ground were a small boy with his head propped on his hands, a little girl, and their dog. The caption read, "In the days before television."

Even as a kid, it hit me that there was once a time when people had other things to do. Centering a main living area around the TV might have mixed up priorities. That comic, funny as it was, became a sort of warning. We realized early on that television could quietly take over the best part of the house, not because it's evil, but because it's easy. It's easy to tune out instead of leaning in.

When we had kids, that *Far Side* comic inspired us to create a different atmosphere that didn't treat the television like an idol to be worshiped. We set out to create a room where conversation could thrive—free from devices, media, and noise—and where Mom and Dad would be predictably present every day. We were not anti-technology; we just wanted our home to have at least one space centered on people, not screens. We wanted a place where ideas could be explored, apologies could be made, and laughter could last longer than a punchline.

We collected furniture that was comfortable, that would seat all of us and then some, and that would allow us to spend as much time together as we wanted. Mom and I had our chairs, which were right beside each other and facing the center of the room. At the perfect distance for hearing an "inside voice" conversation, there was a sofa facing the two chairs, also tilted toward the center of the room. To our left was a large loveseat, perpendicular to the chairs and sofa—and yes, also facing the center of the room. Finally, we had a large ottoman with wheels that could be moved to accommodate two or three others as we conversed into the night. All the furniture was close enough to be conducive for conversation.

We wanted the room to invite connection. Everything about the arrangement said, "We are here. You matter. Let's talk." And talk, we did.

Our living room was *the place* for teaching, listening, laughing, telling stories, and reinforcing our values. In that living room, we could number in the hundreds the times we talked about things that happened at work, church, birthday parties, and other events. It became our family classroom—not the kind with a chalkboard and desks, but the kind where real life got sorted out, one conversation at a time.

We wanted to listen so you all would be more willing to join us. We tried to create a judgment-free zone where you all could speak your minds, give your opinions, and work through your own underdeveloped philosophies of life. We fully understood that we could have failed in this, but we tried. And we knew that trying mattered. Trying meant we showed up. It meant you had somewhere to bring your questions, your doubts, and your half-formed ideas. You didn't need to have it all figured out. You just needed to know that we were there, and that we cared.

We believe that something was taught, reinforced, or debated almost every night, in every living room we had, for over twenty years. We set out to drive home our values primarily in that space. Most of the time, conversations in that room happened after a situation had passed, not in the middle of it. That way, emotions weren't as likely to run high. Timing matters. It's hard to receive wisdom when you're still steaming mad or riding the wave of embarrassment. So we waited. And that waiting created space for grace.

We would bring up situations that were two or three days old and ask, "What could have been done differently?" At that point, we were trying to put on the shelves of your heart more and more copies of the same book: that unwritten book of the values we were trying to instill. We were not trying to script your responses. We were trying to fill your internal library with useful reference points, so when the next challenge came, you had something to draw from.

PRACTICE MAKES PERFECT

"Tell me and I forget, teach me and I remember, involve me and I learn." —Unknown

It was in those various living rooms that we practiced what we taught. We role-played scenarios in the living room so that you would know what to say when someone asked you a predictable question. We didn't expect you to get it right the first time, or even the second. What we cared about was the pattern, the repetition, the effort. Just like athletes run drills and musicians rehearse scales, we believed practicing kindness, respect, and self-control would train your hearts for the moments that mattered.

During the Christmas season, we practiced how to answer the "What is Santa going to bring you this year?" question. We didn't want to crush imaginations or spark awkward moments, but we did want you to speak truth with grace—and do so without making other kids feel foolish. That takes finesse, and finesse doesn't come without practice.

When we were invited to someone's house for dinner, we worked on how to look our hosts in the eye, give them a firm handshake, and speak clearly. We didn't accept shyness the "I don't know what to say to adults" excuse because we knew adults would form impressions quickly. We wanted your kindness, curiosity, and respect to shine through in those first few moments, not just for their sake, but for yours. **Confidence, we found, is often just preparation in disguise.**

That living room was practice for walking away because we didn't allow you to stomp off.

It was also in that living room that we admit we made lots of mistakes. We interrupted you. We corrected and chastised you when you were being open and honest. We should have been better listeners. We were terrible at giving the proverbial microphone to the softer-spoken members of our family. (Audrey and Mom, we didn't give you a chance to speak, did we?) We sometimes allowed you to be mean, and sometimes we were mean ourselves. This is hard to admit, but it's true: Parenting in real time is messy. We wanted to be perfect examples, but instead we became imperfect witnesses to our own need for grace. And if you saw us apologize—truly apologize—then hopefully you learned how to do it, too.

I can remember one time when I was being very judgmental toward one of your friends, and I saw the hurt in Audrey's eyes. She was okay when we talked about values, but when we personally judged someone's appearance, it broke her heart. I apologize for that; I see now that I should have given her more space to share her feelings. Parents have much to learn from their kids, too.

> **WARNING:** *Kids, here is your fourth warning. Always be aware of the quiet ones in your group. They often have the best opinions. Do you know why? Because they spend most of their time listening. In your future family, in a management situation, or with friend groups, be aware of the quiet and reserved members of the group, and* **create** *an opportunity for them to speak. I feel I could have been a better dad if I hadn't dominated the conversation so much and listened more, especially to those who were less likely to impose their will on the conversation. Quiet is not weakness. It's often wisdom dressed as humility. Make space for it. Draw it out. Some of your greatest insights in life*

will come from voices that rarely interrupt, boast, or demand to be heard.

THE GROCERY STORE

The complete opposite of the living room is the grocery store. This is a place in which children of all ages have chosen to work on their skills as beggars and pleaders. They get the best of their worn-out parents as they approach the checkout lines, where all the candy, gum, and treats are perfectly situated at eye-level for any six-year-old to see.

We knew that if the living room was our practice field, the grocery store was game day. If the living room was where we did our homework, the grocery store was where we took our final exam.

It was at the grocery store that we hoped to put into practice everything we were trying to teach at home. It was also one of the places (along with church and the YMCA) that our "failures" were put on display for the entire world to see.

We decided early on that we were not going to bribe you all to do what is right (e.g., "Levi, if you are good today, we might get you a treat when we check out!"). That kind of bribe is empty, and while it often gets you what you want in the moment, it also undermines the careful work of training your children's hearts. Our deepest desire was for you all to act justly and do what's right, not for a reward or for recognition, but *simply because it is right.*

Do you know how much faith we had to have in this philosophy to avoid caving? It would have been *much* easier to offer each of you some token or prize for being marginally better behaved when we went grocery shopping. But I give your mom all the credit: Every other Thursday, you all would make the trip from Sam's Club to Aldi to Walmart to Kroger to get everything on our list at the best possible price. By the end of the day, everyone was exhausted, and Mom was usually at her wit's end. She left the house knowing that she had to be willing to abandon a half-filled cart at Walmart and go home, licking her wounds as she realized we had more work to do before we went out in public again.

It's not that you all were terrible—you were just children being childish. But when you have four kids in a seven-year span and all of them are still at "annoying" ages, it's hard to get them to listen at the same time and behave accordingly.

Eventually, though, you learned the rules. You stopped begging for treats and started helping by finding items on coupons and organizing the grocery cart. Even though you eventually fell in line, we never believed that trying to teach you or reprimand you in public was going to be very fruitful. We made notes, then went back home and addressed the problem there.

OUR ROUND TABLE

The living room was our number one place for instructing, debating, and correcting. The grocery store often served as the public place of humiliation. And the dining room table was the place for more intimate, heartfelt instruction.

FROM MOM: Much was discussed and debated (and hopefully taught) at the dining room table. This was my domain. I wanted to provide time around the table to eat and to live life together. I longed for conversation, for us to tell each other about our day, talk about relationships, and go over evening plans, and for you to learn to help clean up and pitch in. My heart was always so full when my table was also full. Your dad and I *loved* it when you wanted to bring your friends home for dinner. You made me feel good when you bragged about my cooking to your friends. And at the same time, we wanted a place where your friends could sit with us and we could get to know them better.

When there was someone special in your life, I wanted to cook for them. (It was your dad who wanted to grill them!) We knew you had good friends when they would spontaneously offer to set the table or clear it after the meal. We were always so impressed.

That is one of the values that we wanted to instill in you kids: When you are at someone's house, show gratitude. Be helpful. Be respectful. We would *practice* this at home.

FROM DAD: Yes, I would always make you all say, "Thank you, Mom, for a good supper," or something to that effect. She didn't need the ego boost; it was more a way to drive into your subconscious an overall sense of thankfulness toward other people.

At the dining room table, we sat closer together; we were all at eye-level, and we often had guests around the table, too. This was the place where we would ask guests about their life, their family, their hopes and dreams. The dining room table was a place to share more personal feelings about a person or situation. It was more conducive to shorter but heartfelt conversations. It was also the place where battles were raged. Mom and I would often let disagreements continue at the table, as it was a "safe" place out of the public eye, where each person could say their piece and still be loved afterward.

It was the place where Levi and I battled almost to the death over his refusal to eat broccoli (that day, everyone remembers). It was also the place where the F-word was discussed and a huge misunderstanding took place.

After being at work all day, I had not really spent much time with you kids before Mom called us all to the dinner table. The forks and knives made their normal clanging sounds, and there was the occasional thud of a water bottle or glass touching the table after a big gulp.

Out of the blue, Emma, who sat directly to my right, turned her head to me and said, "Dad, Levi said the F-word today."

The background noise of supper stopped.

Every head turned to me.

Mom looked up and gave me "the look."

I looked at Levi as he chewed his food, oblivious to the rage building up in my soul as I thought, "How much do I overreact in this situation?! How could he know this word at his age? Where did he hear it? We homeschool, for crying out loud!" Just before I grabbed him and dragged him to his room by his collar, I took a breath to collect myself. I turned to Emma and said, "Emma, whisper in my ear the word that Levi used today."

She leaned over and whispered, "Dad, he told Mom earlier today that when he didn't get a popsicle after lunch, that was not *fair*!"

I relaxed then, my heart rate dropping back to normal. While it was true that we didn't allow that word or even that sentiment in our house, at least our homeschooled nine-year-old had not used the other F-word at home that day.

> **PRINCIPLE:** *In our house, we focused a lot of our teaching on doing the right thing, even if things did not seem fair. We tried to teach you that things just aren't fair, and we even said that we were never going to try to be fair. Max might get more privileges than Levi at the same age, and we were not going to apologize for that. That was our prerogative, and we had our reasons. So we stressed that life is not fair, and we would interrupt any of you if you started a sentence with "But that's*

not fair!" We did not allow you to say such things. It wasn't helpful.

FROM MOM: I cherished the time around our table the most. Your dad probably preferred the living room, but there is still something special to me about all of us sitting around the table and eating dinner together. As you all know, I might start crying at the table just because it makes me so happy to have everyone gathered around it. I want to take a picture every single time we all sit around the table because of how it makes me feel.

THE CHURCH LOBBY

While you would naturally want your kids to be on their best behavior anywhere, church was the place where we would feel the most pressure, the most embarrassment, and potentially the most perceived judgment. As a pastor's son myself, I felt the pressure to always behave because of that. Now, as a pastor in my own right, I felt even more eyes on our kids.

The people we went to church with were like-minded peers in the same stage of life as us. They were people we loved and shared values with. But they were also the ones who, while not *intentionally* judgy, we couldn't help but feel had their eyes on us while our kids ran around, seemingly out of control. We felt we had to be the most confident in our parenting philosophy at church because that is where we would feel the greatest amount of pressure to be reactive parents, threatening parents, repeating parents, and the like.

So, going back to the living room, we chose a phrase to practice religiously that meant business. When we called out this phrase, all playing stopped, all running stopped, and everyone ran to Mom and Dad's side—*immediately*.

This was a scene taken straight from one of your dad's favorite movies as a teenager: *Young Guns*, starring Emilio Estevez, Charlie Sheen, and Lou Diamond Phillips. In the scene, all these rambunctious, aimless adolescent boys were called to gather together and act as one while being trained by a man who dared to teach them manners and etiquette. The phrase was "Regulators, mount up!"

This became our parental war cry, and to those other parents around us, our calling card. We practiced and practiced and practiced this at home so that when it was time to go to the car after church, all we had to say was "Regulators, mount up!" and you all would come running, regardless of what you were doing.

This was our attempt to stop the cycle of calling you all to leave, then continuing a conversation with friends just to have you kids disappear again. Mom and I decided that we would teach you that you could play and talk until we called you with that phrase. The call of the Regulators meant we were leaving, and if you didn't come right away, you were in trouble.

We used this tactic when you were running around, too. If we saw you running through the lobby around the legs of adults, we used the Regulator call, ended our conversations, and went home. On the way home, we instructed you on how irresponsible and disrespectful it was to run in the presence of the elderly, and how even when church was over and the other kids were running wild, we couldn't let you be the reason that someone fell.

While we had a tactic for corralling you, we knew it was futile to correct you after church was over and everyone was running around, playing, and goofing off. You were with your friends and their parents, and you were either too excited or unwilling to listen in that moment.

The after-church conversations were where we failed the most. We would stand around with all our friends while you and your friends ran wild. We stressed about this exact situation the most, and it was the situation we practiced the most at home. This may seem illogical, but teaching your children about proper behavior *while at church*—when everyone is anxious to go to lunch or go home—is not productive.

Much like the grocery store, church was a test. We either passed or failed. Either way, we discuss your actions at home, make necessary corrections, and—you guessed it—practice even more.

YOUR BEDROOM

The best place for one-on-one instruction and discipline was your bedroom. We could debate things in the living room and we could argue at the dinner table, but when it came to down and dirty reproof, we believed that privacy was key.

WARNING: *In your life as a parent, as a spouse, as an employee, as a boss, and as a fellow member of the human race, never, **ever** forget that everyone is loved by God and is therefore deserving of our general respect. We do **not** have to respect everyone's decisions or lifestyle choices, but we **must** respect each individual person. This is what drove us to not try to correct you at the grocery store but instead to do our disciplining in private: to avoid humiliation. If you use humiliation as a parenting tool, you are weak and lazy. Never let your emotions get the better of you. When you embarrass someone in public, your otherwise productive reproof will go unheard.*

So when a heart-to-heart was necessary, we took you to your bedroom. We knew that potentially meant a spanking or grounding or loss of privilege, and we knew that made you nervous. But we also knew that the only way to teach you was by isolating you from your siblings and giving you a chance to repent in private.

You won't fully understand this until you are parents yourselves. But we remember fondly when we would take you to your room, explain why we did not approve of your behavior, make you acknowledge (truthfully) what you did, and discipline you the way we believed was appropriate at the time. This wasn't because we disciplined you, but because almost every single time, each of you would immediately crawl into our laps while crying and snuggle up to us. In those innocent moments, we could show you how much and how deeply we loved you, even when you had done something unacceptable.

That privilege of sitting on the edge of your bed with you crying in our arms has given us a tiny glimpse of how it feels to God when we repent as sinners. God wants us to live a certain way, and when He disciplines us, it is for our own good. When we realize that and do not turn our back on Him but instead crawl into His lap, we are comforted beyond words.

In fact, the Bible tells us plainly in Romans 5:8:

> *"but God shows his love for us in that while we were still sinners, Christ died for us."*

You see, all of us do wrong. All of us sin. I still do. Your mom does. Even your grandparents do. Even if we desire to always do the right thing, we often fall short of that goal.

FROM DAD: When I was in second grade, my teacher, Mrs. Boykin, had a hard time dealing with me. I was beyond mischievous; I was a terror. I did not listen to a thing she would say, and I was always causing some kind of trouble or stirring up some kind of fight. In my mind, it was funny. No matter how much I could see the frustration on her face, I continued to think everything I was doing was funny, and I did not recognize what I was doing to her and, by extension, all the other kids in my class.

One day, it wasn't funny anymore. I continued pulling all my pranks and causing all sorts of problems, but I was not getting the same enjoyment out of it. After several weeks of dealing with this, I had a conversation with my dad. In the best way I could, I confided in him and told him that all the stuff that used to be funny wasn't funny anymore.

My dad gently explained to me that I was becoming aware of my own sinful heart. This is known as the age of accountability. It is an age or stage of life in which someone becomes aware of their own sinful shortcomings. My dad walked me through the passages in the Bible that talk about sin, how everyone sins (Romans 3:23), and what the ultimate consequences of our sin will be:

"For the wages of sin is death, but the free gift of God is eternal life in Christ Jesus our Lord." (Romans 6:23)

The good news, often called "The Gospel," is that Jesus died on the cross to pay for all our sins, including yours:

"For God so loved the world, that he gave his only Son, that whoever believes in him should not perish but have eternal life." (John 3:16)

As my dad explained all of this to me, I realized, in my own simple, second-grade mind and heart, that I needed to accept the price Jesus had paid for me and ask Him to save me from my sins.

We knelt together at my bed that night. Dad helped me pray to God, and I asked Him to forgive me of my sins. I did not want to cause any more trouble for Mrs. Boykin, for my guilt was heavy. But after that prayer, I was relieved. I repented, and the Holy Spirit came to live in my heart.

I went to school the next day and told Mrs. Boykin about my decision. I don't blame her for not immediately believing me. But to my memory, I didn't cause any more problems for her for the rest of that school year.

In spite of (maybe) behaving for the remainder of that school year, of course I continued to sin and make mistakes. We don't need to be perfect; we only need to be forgiven. I'm grateful I no longer *want* to do the wrong things.

WE ARE WORKING ON IT

Your mom and I adopted a phrase when you all acted foolishly while we were in public. We simply looked at whoever was around us and said, "I apologize on their behalf. We are working on it."

Have you ever watched a parent scold their kids in public? Have you ever looked at the face of a child being berated by their parents in the parking lot or at the checkout counter? How did that make you feel? Did you feel sorry for that child? Did you think poorly of those parents? Usually, parenting in public has very limited benefits.

FROM MOM: Walking away and leaving a full grocery cart in the aisle was always a big fear of mine, but it was something I knew I might have to do to make a point. While I love you all so much, going to the store with all of you was an organizational challenge. Fortunately, your dad and I were on the same page. We were not going to let you whine to get your way.

PURPOSE CHECKLIST

- What changes do you need to make in order to make your values more easily teachable to your kids?

- Do you need to set aside a place for robust, uninterrupted family discussions?

- Do you try to discipline your kids in inappropriate environments?

- Do not bribe your children to behave.

- Be willing to admit your own shortcomings while still parenting to your standards.

VALUES

The Value of Purpose

The Value of Respect

The Value of Diligence

The Value of Self-Discipline

The Value of Humility

The Value of Being a Lifetime Learner

The Value of Generosity

The Value of Marriage

The Value of Faith

The Value of Righteousness

The Value of Words

The Value of Love

The Value of Thinking for Yourself

The Value of Traditions

The Value of Hospitality

The Value of Purity

Chapter 5

ARETHA FRANKLIN SAID IT BEST

*"I'm not concerned with your liking
or disliking me. All I ask is that you
respect me as a human being."*

—JACKIE ROBINSON

THE VALUE OF R-E-S-P-E-C-T

You know that song: "Respect" by Aretha Franklin. It conjures up so much emotion; the way she sang it, you know she meant it.

We may not have sung it, but we meant it, too.

We expected you to show respect. Period. Disrespectfulness is one of the most off-putting characteristics that a child can possess. Everyone notices it. Everyone is repulsed by it. It is not acceptable in any situation—ever! Is it okay to be disrespectful to a teacher? No! To a coach? No! To a stranger at the grocery store? No! To your mom? An emphatic, all-caps NO!

Respect was non-negotiable. It wasn't just a rule; it was a reflection of your character. We believed strongly that if we didn't train it into you early, the world would train it into you later, and much more harshly.

Respect starts at home. Mom and I knew that if we didn't lay down the law at home and require respect from all of you, then we would be doing you a disservice. We would be allowing you to enter the real world with a glaring flaw. Employers immediately notice people who are prone to insubordination just by how respectful or disrespectful they seem in interviews. This is why we always corrected your tone, responses, and attitude. More than anything else, we taught you the *value* of respect.

Yes, tone mattered. The way you said something carried as much weight as what you said. We were listening for attitude, not just words.

Since Mom was at home with you all day, we knew that she would have to be able to control you with her voice. There were times when she was changing a diaper, ironing clothes, using the bathroom, or stirring spaghetti, and she couldn't physically deal with all the situations that would arise with four kids in the house. We knew that training and retraining, correcting and recorrecting to make sure all of you immediately responded to your mom's voice was the only way she would be able to keep the home running.

This is why we practiced at home. This is why we made you respond immediately when one of us called your name. If your mom called for one of you and you didn't respond within one second, whenever possible, one of us would go straight to you and make you respond.

We weren't nitpicking; we were preparing you. When someone speaks to you, it's only respectful to acknowledge them. When you ignore them, it communicates that they don't matter. And that's not how we treat people in our family.

Not responding because you were in the middle of a video game was unacceptable. It would instantly, without recourse or argument, result in us taking that video game away from you. This is also why we chose to require "Yes, ma'am," "No, ma'am," "Yes, sir," and "No, sir," as responses. This was an easy way for us to communicate.

While it may have seemed like Southern tradition, it was really about clarity and civility. We saw those responses as small hinges that swing big doors. They were small habits that helped shape bigger attitudes.

Mom might call from the kitchen, "Audrey!" and Audrey would have to respond immediately, "Yes, ma'am!" instead of "What?" or "Just a minute!" or even nothing. Mom might ask her to come to the kitchen when she had a chance or inquire about her homework or chores. But that immediate response was a respectful way to treat Mom on a day-to-day basis.

We know that not all parents require a "Yes, sir," or "Yes, ma'am," from their kids. But I will say this: Whether a twelve-year-old responds to an adult with a casual "Yeah," or a "Yes, sir," tells you a lot about the values that child was raised with.

A respectful response says, *I'm listening. I understand authority. I've been taught how to respond.* That matters more than you might think.

Which statement do you want from your kids?

FROM DAD: Kids, here's why I acted like a complete, out-of-control moron sometimes. You all remember how I got red-faced, punched the wall, and kicked over chairs if you were ever disrespectful to your mom. I would lay it on thick, overreact, and lose my ever-loving mind. Each time, I would try to raise the intensity level to "panic" or "bonkers" or "nuclear" just to make a point. After my tirade, your mom and I would often walk into our bedroom together, and I would whisper to her, "Did I come on too strong?"

Of course, that wasn't the ideal reaction. But it came from a good intention: protecting the one person who held our whole home together. Sometimes the only way to get your attention was with fire, not because I didn't love you, but because I loved her more. And I needed you to love her too, with your tone, your words, and your attitude.

First-time obedience is a hallmark of respectful kids. On top of immediate response, we also required immediate action. As a parent, there is probably nothing quite as exhausting over ten years as ensuring consistent respect through first-time obedience. If you require it, your kids will respond. But as soon as you relax, they will, too. Make no mistake, this is a respect issue. When you tell your kids to do something and they flatly ignore the command, that calls for swift and painful action! I'm sure you all knew you'd messed up when I heard your mom tell you to do something and you didn't do it right away.

We had a code: *You do what you're told, when you're told—happily.*

This code covered every aspect of respect. You didn't just have to complete a task you were given; you also had to do it right away and with the right attitude.

That last part mattered most. A slammed door is not obedience. A sigh and an eye roll is not obedience. If you do the right thing with the wrong attitude, it will still be wrong.

This was another of our motto we lived by: *Delayed obedience equals disobedience.*

You needed to move when called on to move. For your own benefit—the ability to compete in the real world—you needed to learn this practice. We simply couldn't tolerate disrespectful actions or attitudes. Your elementary school years were especially tough; the training and correcting were relentless, but the value of respect had to be taught.

A major part of management and parenting alike is positive reinforcement. When we saw you (authentically) acting respectful in the outside world, we praised you for it. When you would run ahead and open the door for the older couple entering Chick-fil-A several feet in front of us, we acted like it was the most selfless act known to mankind. We wanted you to know how proud we were when you noticed an opportunity to show others preference and acted on it. It was a way to reinforce the value of respect, of putting others first.

Catch them doing good. That's the principle. If all kids ever hear is correction, they tune out. But when you call out the good, they lean in and learn who they are becoming.

In a terribly selfish world, putting others ahead of your own interests is rare, but it speaks volumes.

> *"Do nothing from selfish ambition or conceit, but in humility count others more significant than yourselves." (Philippians 2:3)*

We believe strongly in this principle: *Service to many leads to greatness.*

It's not the greatness you are seeking; it is what you reap when you sow that service. It's putting others first and showing deep respect that we want to encourage—and the world will reward you.

There are traits we require of you, and now is when we take the time to explain them.

We hammered home the idea of respecting others, and one of the rules we instituted was the "Interruption Rule." That meant that you had to place your hand on our arm when you wanted something while we were speaking to someone on the phone or face to face. This was to teach you that something that seems urgent to you doesn't give you permission to interrupt a conversation between adults.

This led to many, many corrections. Kids are used to running up to a parent, pulling on their pant leg, and saying, "When can we get ice cream next?" or something else unimportant. At home, we had you practice placing your hand on our arm to wait for a break in the conversation. It was a practice rooted in respect for the adults who were talking to each other.

Another rule (that you all found many loopholes around) was that you couldn't ask us to have one of your friends over for the night if you and that friend were standing right in front of us. It was disrespectful to put your parents on the spot and force them to make a quick decision. We told you that if you ever asked us about a sleepover with your friend in front of us, the answer would be an automatic no. This happened once or twice, and we saw the immense disappointment in your faces when you realized you had violated the rule.

After a short season of having you study the rulebook, we noticed that you would make your friends stand a little away from us, but still in direct view of the conversation. Because they could tell what was happening, we were still being put on the spot, so we adjusted the rule to include a five-minute waiting period before we gave an answer. This was all in an effort to teach you to respect others by not putting them in awkward or uncomfortable situations.

Wearing a hat to church was another respect-related conversation, one in which we had to agree to disagree and come up with a compromise. I was a boy who read and followed a lot of military-related movies and books, and I was raised in a home where military-type rules for hat-wearing were enforced, so it was easy for me to accept taking my hat off when entering a building of any kind, especially a church or government building.

Once, Levi wore a hat to church as a teenager, and I scolded him pretty bad for it. He took it off, I assume out of respect for me. But it happened again. And again. Finally, we had a conversation in our living room about hats and respect. He asked, "Dad, why is wearing a hat inside considered disrespectful?"

I said, "It's a military rule, and it's in the Old Testament."

"But why is it disrespectful *today*?"

I paused. "I don't know, exactly. It just is."

"But explain it to me so I understand. In my heart, I do not feel disrespect toward anyone when I walk into church or any other building."

After more back and forth, I finally had to come to the conclusion that taking a hat off at church is a form of respect to me, and that would be as far as it went.

Another sign of respect is avoiding embarrassing someone. It's best to allow someone to save face, so to speak, and keep their dignity.

When we spanked you, we did it behind closed doors so your siblings couldn't watch, because that would have been humiliating. That is a major reason we tried not to yell at you in public. We knew the training ground was at home, and we knew that if we kept scolding you in public, you would begin to feel bitterness toward us. So we saved our scolding for a private space. It was our way of showing respect to you.

> **WARNING:** *In the future, you will be parents, coaches, teachers, and/or bosses, and you will inevitably need to correct someone. Hopefully you know now that doing so in private is the only proper way to do it.*
>
> *"You correct in private and praise in public."*
>
> *Living out this philosophy is a way to show others respect. To people we disagree with, we show respect. To people who are hostile toward us, we show respect. To people who are disrespectful to us in public, we show respect. You must have the self-discipline (see Chapter 7) to do this always, even to people who don't seem "worthy."*

There is another form of respect that we have tried to instill in you, and that is respect toward people in the service industry. Be kind to waitresses. My goodness, I can't believe how some people treat service staff with disdain! They make comments like "Well, there goes their tip!" as if they hold power over a server's head. Basic human decency says that when someone is serving you, you show them the same respect you would want them to show you. People don't need to earn something we owe them by default.

This is known as the Golden Rule: "*Do unto others as you would have them do unto you.*"

Salespeople, receptionists, nurses, and anyone else we come in contact with should be shown a certain level of respect. If we can't do that, then we shouldn't expect it from the world, either.

Here's a different side to the same coin: Don't ask your friends who own a business to give you a discount. If you know the local Chick-fil-A owner, don't go asking for free sandwiches. If you have a friend who's a plumber and you need plumbing work done at your house, don't expect a discount. Respect someone's work.

It's one thing if they want to give you a discount. But you should have respect for those out there making a living as entrepreneurs. Always be willing to pay full price for a product or service, or don't buy it at all.

People never get rich by asking for discounts, and people never go bankrupt for paying full price for a legitimate service.

Respect for others is respect for their Maker. If we believe that everyone was created by God, then everyone is His family, even if our ideas, thoughts, and lives don't always align.

FROM MOM: While this issue was certainly taught at my house, it seems that your dad and his brother (your uncle) might have behaved in such a way that they needed more reminders. This is why your dad brought this value into our home with such fervor. I greatly appreciate the way he prioritized me. I love him for that. It is hard for some people to demand respect for themselves, especially when in the middle of constant power struggles. The fact that he would come home from wherever he was to make sure you all were showing me respect made me feel loved as a wife. Girls, make sure that if you marry, you choose a man who will go out of his way to make sure your kids show you respect. Our house was a much better place because Dad refused to let you talk back or show me any form of disrespect.

RESPECT CHECKLIST

- Are your kids a little disrespectful?
- Do your kids roll their eyes when you tell them to do something?
- Are you setting a good example of respect for them when you encounter people in public?
- Sons, make sure, above all else, that your wives feels loved by you and respected by your kids.
- Respect is not predicated on how others treat you; it is owed by default because you all have the same Maker.

VALUES

The Value of Purpose

The Value of Respect

The Value of Diligence

The Value of Self-Discipline

The Value of Humility

The Value of Being a Lifetime Learner

The Value of Generosity

The Value of Marriage

The Value of Faith

The Value of Righteousness

The Value of Words

The Value of Love

The Value of Thinking for Yourself

The Value of Traditions

The Value of Hospitality

The Value of Purity

Chapter 6

THE STORY OF PEYTON MANNING

"Do or not do. There is no try."

—YODA

"I'm a great believer in luck, and I find the harder I work, the more I have of it."

—THOMAS JEFFERSON

THE VALUE OF DILIGENCE

I (Dad) grew up in the shadow of Neyland Stadium near Knoxville, Tennessee. Neyland is where the University of Tennessee plays their home football games. Growing up when and where I did, you really had no choice but to be a huge fan of the Big Orange. If you lived in East Tennessee during that time, you know that college football wasn't just something people watched on weekends; it was a full-season commitment. People planned weddings, vacations, and even church service times around the Volunteers' schedule. It was more than a sport; it was an identity, a community, and a tradition rolled into one.

Tennessee was fun to watch, and they had years when they could conceivably win any game they played. The '90s had particularly good years, and 1994 was the beginning of something special. That was the freshman year of the one and only Peyton Manning. He wasn't just a good quarterback; he was thoughtful, composed, and willing to do the hard, unglamorous work of preparation. People recognized that early on.

With his dad playing college football at the University of Mississippi and professional football in New Orleans, it was unlikely Tennessee would land the heralded Manning as a recruit. Still, he signed with them, and the next several years were magical for any fan of the Vols. At the end of his senior season, Peyton Manning was the most decorated college athlete and the most anticipated new entry into the NFL in the country.

He was selected as the first pick in the NFL draft and signed one of the largest contracts ever signed by a rookie at the time.

During his entire career at Tennessee, Peyton graciously made himself available to the local sports media and was often interviewed on the local radio stations. As his career at Tennessee ended and he was planning to begin his move to the NFL, he granted the local media another interview. He talked to local sports radio host Mike Keith, and they discussed his college career, his new NFL assignment, and his big contract.

As the interview wound down, Keith asked Manning one last question: "Peyton, you just signed one of the largest contracts in NFL history. What are you going to do with all that money?"

Without hesitation, Peyton replied, *"Earn it."*

Those two words have never left me. They held weight. They held humility. But most of all, they held responsibility. In a world where many people expect rewards without effort, that answer was deeply refreshing.

As I write this chapter about hard work, diligence, and industriousness, I can't get over how I felt when I heard Peyton Manning say that.

When we raised you, we wanted you to have a deep sense of work ethic and to work at the right things for the right reasons. We wanted you to "earn" your place in the world.

This was not about your personal, intrinsic value but about your contribution. There is dignity in work, especially when it is done with integrity and purpose.

Of course, you don't have to do anything to earn our love and support. As our children, we will always love you, no matter what. You are the apple of our eye. You can fail over and over again, and we will still love you.

There is a difference between unconditional love and earned respect. In this house, you are unconditionally loved. But out there in the world, what you build will often depend on how hard you're willing to work.

In our house, we forgive and learn. But that isn't the case outside of our home. This world, unfortunately, is diabolical, and those who are lazy, those who pretend to get things done but don't, and those who *expect* things from others get trampled. We wanted you to be hardworking, dependable, and diligent.

In fact, the word "diligent" was always important to us. We define a diligent person as someone who (1) works hard (2) on the right things (3) at the right time. This is our three-pronged approach to completely defining the word "diligence."

How do we define hard work? Effort is one key. Going the extra mile to actually complete a task is another. That means not allowing threads of laziness, complacency, or excuses to keep you from doing what you are supposed to do.

> *"Talent is cheaper than table salt. What separates the talented individual from the successful one is a lot of hard work." —Stephen King*

You'll never regret outworking people. Even if the outcomes vary, the character it builds is unmatched.

THE FIRST PART OF OUR THREE-PRONGED DEFINITION IS SIMPLY WORKING HARD.

This value of diligence, hard work, and industriousness first was obvious in the way we required you to do daily chores without pay. We were not going to pay you an allowance, and we were going to require you to do daily, age-appropriate chores as a contributing member of our household. Hopefully, seeing yourselves as contributing members of the household would translate, one day, into you being contributing members of society. That was the purpose. That was the goal.

These were some of the age-appropriate chores we made you do:

- Age 2+ — Clean up room; put dirty clothes in hamper

- Age 5+ — Return washed silverware to the appropriate drawer (be careful with knives!); set table for meals (parents can place the plates on the table and the five-year-old can place the silverware and napkins)

- Age 7+ — Take out trash; load the dishwasher or wash dishes (depending on height); light yard work (pick up sticks, pull weeds); help with meal prep by stirring ingredients (at one point in our home, we didn't have an ice maker, so one chore we gave our seven-year-olds was to fill the ice trays and place them in the freezer)

- Age 8+ — Wash, dry and fold towels; wash the car; roll the trash can out to the road for pickup; unload the dishwasher (depending on height); sweep the floors; change sheets on own bed; clean toilets; vacuum

- Age 10+ — Make own meals (sandwiches, cereal, microwaveable items); use Clorox wipes to wipe down bathroom sinks; clean mirrors in bathrooms

- Age 12+ — Wash, dry, fold, and put away own clothes; use oven for supervised meal prep (cheese toast, pizza, etc.)

The point is, children are much more capable than we might think. If you live on a farm or have pets, you know that kids can be very helpful with feeding animals or collecting eggs.

We often underestimate what kids can do. When given the chance, most will rise to meet a reasonable challenge, especially if the expectations are clear.

FROM MOM: You must be willing to exercise patience in teaching your children to do chores instead of caving and doing them yourself. I know I frustrated your dad when I allowed you kids to make your own breakfasts or lunches. There was peanut butter and jelly all over the counter, bread left out, dirty knives and messy countertops and sticky hands and everything else. That's the price you must pay to give your kids the confidence to do things themselves, even if imperfectly. The dividends pay out much, much later. You can all take care of yourselves now, and that's priceless to me.

This is why when you had to unload the dishwasher every day and you threw the Tupperware into a cabinet willy-nilly, we would make you come back and fix it. This is why when you did laundry, we made you finish what you started instead of expecting us to finish it for you. Our desire was to teach you work ethic at home before you entered the workforce. And we expected you to enter the workforce early.

WORKING FOR CHICK-FIL-A

We have lots of friends who are owners and operators at various Chick-fil-A restaurants across the country, and they always talked about having their kids work in their store from an early age. So when Max was around twelve, we asked to speak to the owner of our local Chick-fil-A, Ben Prine, to get him a job.

We stood in the dining room and chatted for about thirty minutes as I explained our plan to him. We wanted each of our kids to begin working at the earliest age allowable by our state, which was fourteen. We asked if we could count on him to give them employment so that they could learn to work for someone else at an early age. Here, they would learn the responsibilities of having others depend on them, keeping their uniforms clean, and managing their time around work.

Obviously, Ben became a great friend to us. He has been gracious and generous to all of you. Just as we discussed in our first conversation, each of you started work right after your fourteenth birthday.

Having that job was not just about income. It was about influence, structure, and growth. Chick-fil-A was your first chance to see how effort and responsibility could change the way others viewed you. It was where you started learning to carry yourselves like people who could be trusted.

As I have always said, at your age (or any age, really), it's not about how much money you make but about how you manage the money that you do make.

When you all started working at Chick-fil-A, we knew that you would experience the pressure of serving the public and the friction of having friends at work without spending all your time goofing off. We expected you to struggle with your time management, and we knew there would be things you just didn't like about working in fast food.

And yes, there were hard days. There were frustrating shifts, rude customers, and times when you didn't want to clock in. But that's the point. Work isn't always supposed to feel fun. It's supposed to feel worthwhile.

However, there were also tons of surprises. One of those was your sense of pride in learning a new skill and becoming the best in the store at it. It was fun for us to hear your stories about the drive-thru and how you had an idea that helped the whole store. There is something so satisfying about watching your child gain confidence not because they were praised, but because they knew they had mastered a real skill.

Another thing we didn't see coming was the way having a paycheck would impact all of you. We had spent many hours doing money management training at home, and while I am sure that was worthwhile, it was only theory. When you started getting paid, it became practice. We set up checking and savings accounts for you at the local bank, we had you download the bank app on your phones, and we got you debit cards. Now you had (some) control over your income and what to do with it.

Suddenly, decisions that once felt hypothetical became real. You began to see how five dollars here or twenty dollars there added up. You also began to recognize that each purchase was a choice between instant gratification and longer-term goals.

Suddenly, you had to grow up as you learned about how much it really cost to eat at Taco Bell five days in a row. It would have taken us years and years to teach you all the things you learned in a matter of months of having a job with direct deposit, having access to those funds via debit card, and being able to see the number in your account change in real time. We didn't realize the true impact having a job at fourteen would have on your money management skills. You began to understand that working hard wasn't just for someone else's benefit. It gave you options, autonomy, and a sense of control over your own future.

One final surprise: Being part of a multigenerational team, you were colleagues with people in their teens, twenties, thirties, forties, fifties, and sixties. This meant you worked alongside people who did not think the same way you did, who needed a paycheck to make car payments or mortgage payments. You got to see the public in all their glory: angry at getting cold fries or a Diet Coke instead of a Dr Pepper. Your colleagues handled those challenges in different ways, and you had a front-row seat for all of it. People were depending on you to show up for your shift, and you would sometimes be asked to cover a coworker's shift when you didn't want to. Working a real job without real-world problems allowed you to learn the skills and values that constitute hard work.

This exposure was one of the hidden gifts of your experience. You didn't just learn about tasks; you learned about people. You saw grace and stress, compassion and selfishness, all in one environment. And you learned to manage yourself in the middle of it all.

Working hard is not just for work. It's important in every endeavor of life. On an athletic team, working hard is often synonymous with the word "hustle." It was not okay to practice or play halfheartedly.

One day, Emma was playing soccer for a U12 team. Our community didn't have a coed or even girls-only U12 teams at the time, so she played on a boys-only team. She held her own against boys who were just starting to outgrow, outrun, and outkick her. That season, she had to work hard and hustle for everything.

When she was the only girl playing in the entire tournament, she worked so hard and hustled so much that parents from the visiting team began commenting on "that blonde girl with the ponytail." Some said that she shouldn't be there, that the boys would hurt her. Some suggested that she was taking a spot from some other boy. Others thought that as the game went on, she would be outmuscled and eventually need to be benched. But none of them knew Emma and her work ethic.

Eventually, she won over those naysayers and impressed all the parents. At one point in the second half, Emma ran full speed to stop the ball from going out of bounds and retain possession for her team. But a much larger, taller, and heavier boy had the same idea. A collision seemed inevitable. Then suddenly, Emma dropped her shoulder and drove her body into his, and that boy went spilling off toward the parking lot like a Texas tumbleweed.

Like any proud dad, I immediately leaped into the air and yelled, "That's my daughter! That's my girl on the field! Whoopee!"

It wasn't Emma's aggression I praised; it was her grit. She had worked for every ounce of strength and skill she brought to that game. That moment didn't come from luck. It came from hustle.

As a family, we love sports, and we believe that participating in a sport is a great way to learn the value of hard work. It didn't take long for all of you to realize that the extra work you put into your sport was worth the effort. Scheduled practice wasn't enough; you had to go home and work on what the coach wanted you to work on, over and over and over again.

Hard work beats talent every time.

We have watched this play out time and time again. Kids would start out with superior talent but do nothing to cultivate it, and it wouldn't take long for their hardest-working teammates to surpass them and become the new MVPs.

This was never more obvious than when Levi chose to take up lacrosse as a junior in high school. He had never even held a lacrosse stick before, but the school didn't cut anyone who tried out, so he made the team anyway. He rode the bench his junior year, barely getting into any games. But all I heard from his coaches were things like "He works harder than anyone on the team," and "If I had a team full of Levis, we would never lose," and "Levi asks so many questions; his willingness to learn will get him far."

Levi always stayed after practice to learn more. He asked teammates to help him train. Then, in the off-season, he created a drill-heavy routine that forced him to learn the fundamentals in double time, and he didn't take a day off the entire summer and fall. When spring rolled around in his senior year, he was immediately promoted to starter over boys who had been playing lacrosse since elementary school. His work ethic had paid off. At the end of the season, the coaches awarded him the coveted "spirit award," which was given each year to the player with the biggest heart and the best work ethic.

We have always believed that no matter what curveballs life throws at you, your ability to buckle down and get to work will push you to the top of your chosen field. In athletics, you got to see that happen almost in real time: Emma in soccer, Levi in lacrosse, Max in jujitsu, and Audrey in cheerleading and weight lifting. In practically no time at all, you excelled because you were diligent in your preparation.

That transformation didn't require fancy training or special connections. It required showing up and repeating the basics until they were no longer difficult.

Once you start practicing diligence, people can count on you. At the same time, this puts more pressure on you because people start relying on you. Have you ever had an undependable friend who no one expected anything from? I know you have. There is an emptiness that comes with knowing you can't be counted on. But the pressure that comes with being dependable is good. It's an adult, mature pressure, a prerequisite to leadership.

Dependability may feel heavy at times, but it is also how trust is built. And trust, once earned, becomes a doorway to meaningful responsibility and influence.

THE SECOND ASPECT OF DILIGENCE IS WORKING ON THE THINGS THAT MATTER.

We saw this play out in four-year-old soccer. Coaches in the league would spend an inordinate amount of practice time on the strategy of soccer and not nearly enough time on the fun and fundamentals of kicking and running. Four-year-olds do not comprehend spacing strategy, no matter how well-versed and passionate the coach may be. Diligence includes the wisdom to prioritize.

How many people do you know who have the uncanny ability to waste time by working hard on completely irrelevant and meaningless things? Seriously, how do you impact the world by vacuuming under your bed every single week? We joke a lot when we don't want to do something: "I'm so sorry, I can't. I have to organize my sock drawer." And yet, so many people insist on organizing their metaphorical sock drawers anyway.

Busyness does not always mean productivity. Some people use busywork as a way of avoiding harder, more important work. It feels like progress, but it's really procrastination.

Granted, what I find important may not be important to you, and vice versa. But we should be able to agree that scrolling social media is not nearly as impactful as physical exercise.

Kids, there will be times when your mom or I might think you're not working on the right things while you think you are. Perhaps we will often disagree. But always consider whether you are only choosing low-impact activities over high-impact ones because the latter seem harder.

The real question to ask yourself is this: "Am I doing this because it matters, or because it is easier than the thing that actually matters?" The answer may be uncomfortable, but it can guide you back to what counts.

Diligence is therefore working hard on the right things.

THE THIRD ASPECT OF BEING DILIGENT IS WORKING HARD ON THE RIGHT THINGS AT THE *RIGHT TIME*.

Every single time your mom and I were about to go out of town for a long trip, she would decide she wanted to take on a big project, like painting the bathroom. We joke all the time about choosing to do something important at the absolute worst time. The real wisdom of diligence is the ability to choose what to work hard on when it actually needs to be worked on. I'm sure painting a room was the right thing to do, but the timing was still wrong.

Sometimes doing the right thing isn't a one-time deal; sometimes it's something you do every day.

This is the definition of consistency. When you are a diligent worker, you are a consistent worker. You show up today *and* tomorrow. As Andy Frisella often says in his book *75 Hard*, you must "master the mundane." Someone who is diligent is willing to do the boring work over and over again.

Consistency is not exciting. It does not always produce fireworks. But it is how trust, skill, and success are built. Most people fail not because they do not know what to do, but because they cannot keep doing it consistently.

Admittedly, on the subject of diligence, hard work, and industriousness, we failed in many ways—most of all in how we managed your music lessons. All of you took lessons to learn an instrument (piano, guitar, or drums), and your practice with those instruments was the opposite of diligent.

It was inconsistent, halfhearted, and undependable. We do not know exactly why we let this go, but we did. For that reason, all of you have significantly less ability playing an instrument you love than you should.

This is one of those parenting regrets that lingers. We didn't expect you to become professional musicians, but we know what consistent effort could have done for you, and we let it slip.

As parents, we didn't live up to our own standards of hard work, and now all of you have shared an interest in starting lessons again as adults. You know you could already be playing at a much higher level if only you had practiced consistently, but you didn't. Sometimes, we fail in our plans to be good parents and good workers.

There is no hiding from that truth. But we hope it also serves as a reminder that even diligence itself must be practiced, modeled, and sometimes relearned.

DILIGENCE CHECKLIST

- What do you need to do today to become more dependable, more reliable, more consistent, and more hardworking?

- When you work hard, are you focusing on the things that matter?

- Do you need to get better at timing the "when" of your hard work?

- Do not make excuses. Accept responsibility for shortcomings and commit to doing better.

- Be patient with others who are not hard workers. Keep your own standards high, but show others grace.

VALUES

The Value of Purpose

The Value of Respect

The Value of Diligence

The Value of Self-Discipline

The Value of Humility

The Value of Being a Lifetime Learner

The Value of Generosity

The Value of Marriage

The Value of Faith

The Value of Righteousness

The Value of Words

The Value of Love

The Value of Thinking for Yourself

The Value of Traditions

The Value of Hospitality

The Value of Purity

Chapter 7

WHO'S GOING TO DO THE WORK FOR YOU?

> *"We are what we repeatedly do. Excellence,*
> *then, is not an act, but a habit."*
>
> —WILL DURANT

THE VALUE OF SELF-CONTROL AND SELF-DISCIPLINE

Fitness trainer and social media influencer Ryan Fischer recently posted on Instagram the following piece of wisdom:

Mediocrity doesn't announce itself.

It hides in skipped workouts.
In late alarms and excuses.
In one "I'll do it tomorrow" after another.

You don't just beat it once.
You battle it every day.

The weapon?

Discipline. Showing up when comfort whispers, "Rest."

Be ruthless with your habits.
Demand better from yourself.

Because if you don't crush mediocrity…
it will quietly crush you.

That quote hits hard because it's true. Mediocrity doesn't come crashing through the door. It sneaks in, one missed chore, one ignored alarm, one indulgent excuse at a time. The drift into average is silent but powerful, and you must be disciplined enough to push back.

There is no doubt that taking daily action is more important than setting goals. At the beginning of every Olympics, every sporting event, or every election, all participants have the same goal. It's not the goal that's the key; it's the persistence, the discipline, the self-control, and the self-denial that create the habits. Routines create winners.

Everyone wants the result, but few are willing to commit to the daily grind required to get there. Goals are the spark, while discipline is the fuel.

There is no question that control and discipline are among the most persistent and taxing jobs of a parent. Before you could achieve self-control and self-discipline as adults, we had to use control and discipline to make you do things.

I mean, when you were still very young, we even had to make you go to the bathroom!

"Levi, do you need to go potty before we get in the car to go to church?"

"Emma, your soccer game is twenty minutes away from here. Do you need to go to the bathroom before we go?"

"Audrey, use the bathroom before you go to bed."

"Max, it isn't smart to drink so much water before a long car trip. Put that down and go pee before we leave."

This is only a taste of what most parents do all day long.

"Put that down!"

"Stop hitting her!"

"Go back to bed!"

"Stop playing with the light switch!"

"Go take your plate to the sink!"

"Did you wash your uniform? Remember you have a game tomorrow."

"Be sure to set your alarm. You have to get up early."

"I guess you didn't set your alarm. It's a good thing I came in here to wake you up."

"I thought you were awake; now you're running late. Get up and get dressed."

"I was just in here! I thought you were getting up. Did you go back to sleep?!"

"Hurry and get your clothes on. You aren't going to have time for breakfast."

"I told you this morning to unload the dishwasher."

"No, do it right now, not when you feel like it."

"I told you not to leave food in your room! Clean this up. Now we have to go get a mousetrap!"

"Practice the piano, please."

"Your grandmother gave you a gift; be sure to thank her."

"Replace the toilet paper roll when you finish it."

"I don't remember telling you that you could watch TV."

"Finish folding your clothes."

"This is why you don't leave a glass of milk in your room for three days."

"Audrey, you can't just get out of the shower without drying off; it leaves a ton of water on the floor for the next person to deal with."

"Boys, leave Audrey alone and just mop it up yourself."

"Levi, quit telling Audrey to stop singing."

"If I've told you once, I've told you a thousand times: Stop chewing with your mouth open."

"Emma, you shouldn't say that about someone. Even if it's true, it's not nice."

"Max, you're driving too fast. Slow down."

"Audrey, did you reply to that email from school?"

"Emma, did you apply for that internship?"

"Boys, I know you were invited to that wedding. Did you RSVP?"

"Audrey, will you please help your mom with dinner?"

"Kids, did you know next Sunday is Mother's Day?"

Controlling and disciplining your kids is truly a full-time job. When you start to feel your kids transitioning to self-control and self-discipline, that's a win for your parent score. Guiding your children toward true self-control warrants a pat on the back.

It won't come with fanfare. No one gives you a ribbon when your child gets up on time without being told to. But inside, you feel the shift, a tiny miracle that says, "It's working."

But boy, is it hard! There are times when we still feel all four of you need nudging, coaching, and straight-out parenting. But the majority of the time, we feel you are mostly independent. We still give reminders, but we don't feel we have to as often. Your moments of independence are our quiet rewards for years of consistent guidance.

This process of turning control into self-control must be a parental priority. Telling one of your kids to go unload the dishwasher right away is one thing. Telling them to do it today and then trusting that they will is another thing entirely. In the latter case, they will inevitably procrastinate, and you will eventually remind them. That's when you find out they completely forgot the assignment, despite you stressing it all day. You'll then feel torn between two instincts: to give up and do it yourself, or to double down and reinforce the boundary. The former is easier. The latter is wiser.

> *"It's the job that's never started as takes longest to finish."* —J.R.R. Tolkien

> *"The great end of life is not knowledge but action."* —*Thomas Henry Huxley*

Parenting requires patience. It may take you several tries to teach your kids how to put the dishes away properly and promptly (all while they roll their eyes and say "I know," a frustration every parent knows well), but eventually, they will start doing it themselves without needing constant reminders.

There are few things more satisfying then when your child wanders through the kitchen, notices that the dishwasher needs to be unloaded, and *chooses* to unload it themselves. That's the parenting equivalent of winning the Publishers Clearing House sweepstakes.

It's a moment of such rare beauty that parents often don't know how to respond. We smile, we quietly celebrate, and then we pretend like it's totally normal. But inside? We are doing a victory lap.

In short, a child's transition from control to self-control is a big deal for parents.

Likewise, self-discipline is perhaps one of the most valuable skills for making something of yourself. Getting out of bed to go to the gym when you don't have to, day after day, is a skill that few people today have.

It's not about the exercise, but about the mindset. The willingness to act when no one is forcing you to is the foundation of maturity.

Turning down a piece of cake because you have nutrition goals is a level of self-discipline that few have. That choice reveals your priorities in the moment. Self-control is not about deprivation; it's about direction.

Rising early for Bible study before going to the gym is an impressive form of self-guidance.

It's important to know this:

No one is going to do the work for you.

Not your parents. Not your teachers. Not your friends. Even the most supportive people in your life cannot carry your discipline for you.

Learning self-discipline, then, is imperative for living a life of purpose and fulfillment rather than a life of disappointment. The world will always make space for someone who consistently does good work. Excellence over time opens doors that talent alone cannot.

"Do you see a man skillful in his work? He will stand before kings." (Proverbs 22:29)

Self-control and self-discipline also keep you from making life-altering mistakes. Mistakes will always be made. Get used to that. But the worst ones can be avoided by showing self-control.

Marriages all over the world would be saved if spouses (mostly men) would have the self-awareness, self-discipline, and self-guidance to never have a solitary, intimate conversation with another person they find attractive. This is how affairs start. Avoiding temptation is a form of self-control that would benefit the world. Affairs do not begin with betrayal; they begin with drifting, with rationalization, with tiny compromises that stack up. It takes enormous strength to draw lines early and honor them.

This also goes for men who watch pornography. Do you have the self-control to view your computer, phone, and TV in public so you don't have the opportunity to go down that dark and evil path? When you are feeling lonely and vulnerable, can you be disciplined enough to go for a run, do push-ups, or call your parents, instead of being lured down that road that leads to destruction? When you are at the gym, do you have the self-control to avert your glance from the young ladies who are looking for attention? This is not about shame. It is about vigilance. Protecting your integrity requires intention. When you know your weaknesses, guard against them. When you know your tendencies, redirect them.

What about shopping? When you *know* you need to save money but you feel bored, can you keep yourself from going to your favorite clothing store? Can you make yourself drive straight home rather than checking out that advertised sale at Old Navy?

One of the primary tenets of self-control is the acknowledgment of failure. Just like the dishwasher example, it takes years or even decades to find the right formula to become truly disciplined. Some people are disciplined about some things, but no one is disciplined about everything. Self-control is a cycle of noticing, adjusting, trying again, and moving forward without quitting.

Everything we've covered so far—marriage, parenting, nutrition, Bible study, personal development, entrepreneurship, gym attendance, church attendance, cleaning schedules, school, cell phone habits, and social media limits—is only a fraction of what requires true discipline to master.

Bottom line: Teaching yourself to be disciplined takes a lot of time.

> *"We must all suffer from one of two pains: the pain of discipline or the pain of regret. The difference is discipline weighs ounces while regret weighs tons."* —*Jim Rohn*

You will not wake up one day as an instant master. But you can wake up today and begin practicing, one small choice at a time.

As parents, we do our kids a *huge* disservice by not expecting them to demonstrate self-control and self-discipline early in life. Doing your kids' work for them doesn't do anyone any good in the long run.

Teach them how to do it.

Make a schedule for them to do it.

Hold them to the schedule.

Praise or correct based on the schedule.

Teach them that the better they get, the more you will trust them.

Actually show them that you trust them.

Encourage them along the way.

And finally, let them go.

SELF-DISCIPLINE AND SELF-CONTROL CHECKLIST

- How are you at helping your kids transition from parental control to self-control?

- Are you willing to put in the time every day to teach your kids with the hope they will one day "get it"?

- What changes need to be made so your kids can take on more responsibility and "own" parts of their lives?

- Watching your kids sink in the pool of self-discipline is painful, but it is equally wonderful to see them swim. Do not falter. It does get better.

- Self-discipline and self-control are struggles that everyone faces. Encourage without fail, but show grace.

VALUES

The Value of Purpose

The Value of Respect

The Value of Diligence

The Value of Self-Discipline

The Value of Humility

The Value of Being a Lifetime Learner

The Value of Generosity

The Value of Marriage

The Value of Faith

The Value of Righteousness

The Value of Words

The Value of Love

The Value of Thinking for Yourself

The Value of Traditions

The Value of Hospitality

The Value of Purity

Chapter 8

BECOME A MONSTER

*"It's better to be a warrior in a garden
than a gardener in a war."*

—Miyamoto Musashi

*"There is no limit to the amount of good you
can do if you don't care who gets the credit."*

—Ronald Reagan

THE VALUE OF HUMILITY

One of the most intriguing interviews I have ever seen changed my mind about what it means to be humble and meek. Most of us grow up hearing that humility is about being quiet and soft-spoken, about not drawing too much attention to yourself. But what if that's only part of the story? What if true humility is not weakness but controlled strength?

On the podcast *The Joe Rogan Experience*, Joe Rogan interviewed the famous psychologist Jordan Peterson. At one point, they began discussing the concept of meekness, a word often used synonymously with humility. It's worth sharing the transcript for the moment when Peterson "redefines" the word "meek" (edited for clarity):

PETERSON:

Well, the other thing I've been telling young men … is I read this New Testament line, well, decades ago, and I could never understand it.

It's the line "*the meek shall inherit the earth.*" And I thought, there's something wrong with that line. It just doesn't make sense to me. *Meek* just doesn't seem to me to be a moral virtue.…

But I was looking through these sayings … and that was one of them, "*the meek shall inherit the earth.*" But I've been using this site called Bible Hub, and it's very interesting.…

So you have a biblical line, and then they have like three pages of commentary on each line. And so, because people have commented on every verse in the Bible … you can look and see all the interpretations and all the translations, and get some sense of what the genuine meaning might be. And in the line "*the meek shall inherit the earth,*" *meek* is not a good translation.

...[The] word has moved in the three hundred years or so since it was translated. What it means is this: *"Those who have swords and know how to use them, but keep them sheathed, will inherit the world."* And that's another thing I've been telling people.

ROGAN:

Yeah, no kidding. That's a lot different.

PETERSON:

And so, one of the things I tell young men ... is that you should be a *monster*. ...[E]veryone says, well, you should be harmless, virtuous. You shouldn't do anyone any harm. You should sheath your competitive instinct. You shouldn't try to win. You know, you don't want to be too aggressive. You don't want to be too assertive. You want to take a back seat and all of that. ...[No], wrong. You should be a *monster*, an absolute *monster*, and then you should learn how to control it.

That idea flips the traditional understanding of humility on its head. You don't need to lack strength or shrink back. You don't need to choose personal weakness. Yes, biblically speaking, Jesus is strong *through* our weakness. From a Christian standpoint, managing these contrasting views is difficult.

Humility doesn't mean being a doormat.

Meekness is not virtuous if you are unable to do any harm at all. If you are truly harmless, according to Peterson, you have no real virtue. Your inability to win is not a virtue. That line is critical. A person who is weak and nonthreatening is not humble. They are simply unable to act. True humility begins when you have options, when you are strong enough to choose restraint.

Wow! This is *exactly* what we wanted to teach all of you. Win! Strive to win! Work hard to win! But by controlling your "monster within," so to speak, **you choose to be humble rather than humbled**. Being humbled means the world knocks you down. Being humble means you voluntarily step back, even when you have the right to take center stage. The former is forced. The latter is chosen.

To choose to be humble is to live a life in which you do not take your own accomplishments or talents or anything else too seriously.

> *"Let another praise you, and not your own mouth; a stranger, and not your own lips."*
> *(Proverbs 27:2)*

There will always someone who is better, stronger, faster, smarter, richer, or wiser than you. As long as you don't aim to always be the best at whatever you do, you are choosing to be humble.

Humility begins when you recognize that you are not the standard. There is always room to grow, always someone to learn from, always a place to serve. We serve a risen Savior, and He is the standard. If you do not *choose* to be humble, you will inevitably be humbled by someone else.

Recall this conversation I (Dad) witnessed once: Max had been putting off getting a permanent tag on his vehicle, even though his temporary tag had expired. When Emma asked him about it, he brushed her off. She said, "You better get that fixed or you'll get a ticket." Max rolled his eyes and said, "How do you know?"

What he did not know at the time was that Emma was in the middle of a three-month internship with the local police department. On ride-alongs, she had seen people get pulled over for expired tags. Needless to say, once Max found this out, his attitude changed.

The real lesson Max learned that day was about assumptions. We should never be so confident in our own perspective that we dismiss someone else's experience.

We never really know what other people know or what they have been through. If you look down on someone, it can come back to bite you—often much worse than a brief moment of embarrassment in front of your younger sibling. Life has a way of humbling the proud. It is far better to start from a place of respect and curiosity than one of arrogance and presumption.

When you have no skills, no work ethic, and no success, it's pretty easy to be "meek." But the choice to put others first (see the principles of respect in Chapter 5), to serve others, to willingly allow yourself to be used when you have the power to stop it—that is humility.

> *"Do nothing from selfish ambition or conceit, but in humility count others more significant than yourselves." (Philippians 2:3)*

Real humility costs something. It's the choice to value others above your own desire for attention or control.

Levi, a prime example of this is the thermostat in your home. You bought the house, you remodeled it, and you maintain it. But some of your roommates want to control the temperature in it. You have the right to set the rules in your own house. But by *choosing* your roommates' comfort over yours, you are, in effect, exercising humility for the sake of harmony and unity.

So what is the benefit of humility? Do you not just get taken advantage of?

That is a fair question. It can feel like humility puts you at risk. After all, the loudest people often get the spotlight. The most assertive people often get ahead. But humility is a long game. It builds trust. It strengthens relationships. It sustains success.

Indeed, arrogance is wildly unattractive, while confidence is appealing. The difference between arrogance and confidence is your willingness to be quietly humble. Confidence is walking down the street, standing up straight, and knowing that you can defend yourself. Arrogance is picking a fight because you *want* to defend yourself. Confidence says, "I can." Arrogance says, "I must prove it." That distinction affects how people receive you, how they work with you, and whether they want to follow you.

FROM MOM: I have struggled with how to parent you all in this. All of you have accomplished so much, and I have constantly pressed you to "speak life." I always wanted you to believe in yourselves, and I never allowed you to put yourselves down. Anytime you would say "I can't" or "I'm not good enough,", I would cut you off. Speaking life is critical, and negative self-talk can be very damaging. But I never knew exactly how to humble you when it felt like you were bragging. This is a difficult balance to strike: I liked it when you said positive things about yourselves, but I didn't want you to say those same things in public. I wanted you to believe, but not boast.

This is one of the trickiest lines to walk in parenting. You want your kids to walk tall, but not to talk over others. You want them to recognize their gifts, but not rely on them for approval. There is no perfect formula, but it's worth the effort to find that balance.

As we discussed in the last chapter, it takes a great deal of self-control to be humble—unless you lack self-respect. We wanted you all to be competent, strong, intelligent, secure, and confident, but we tried to teach you to keep your achievements and skills to yourself. Bragging is repulsive, but that does not mean you need to hide who you are. You only need to carry yourselves with grace. Share your gifts when someone asks; otherwise, just keep building in private.

HUMILITY CHECKLIST

- How do you raise someone who is humble but not insecure?
- How do you raise someone who is confident but not overconfident?
- How do you raise a leader with the maturity and humility to be a follower when necessary?
- Humility coupled with inner confidence is attractive.
- You don't need to be a pushover to be humble.

...und
...id not of ...which
...id I do, done; you mus...
...caving you ...you must
...d & do, have real feeling commence... this mos...
...my ...you my approached...
...to offer. Caroline I am s...
...ears from perceived not su...
...that I have nervous are...
moment love...
Caroline My dearest Car...
tears...

VALUES

The Value of Purpose

The Value of Respect

The Value of Diligence

The Value of Self-Discipline

The Value of Humility

The Value of Being a Lifetime Learner

The Value of Generosity

The Value of Marriage

The Value of Faith

The Value of Righteousness

The Value of Words

The Value of Love

The Value of Thinking for Yourself

The Value of Traditions

The Value of Hospitality

The Value of Purity

Chapter 9

A VOLKSWAGEN'S ENGINE IS IN THE BACK

"I have no special talent. I am only passionately curious."

—ALBERT EINSTEIN

"Shall I tell you the secret of the true scholar? It is this: every man I meet is my master in some point, and in that I learn of him."

—RALPH WALDO EMERSON

"The only true wisdom is knowing you know nothing."

—SOCRATES

THE VALUE OF BEING A LIFETIME LEARNER

You must be a lifetime learner to make a real *lifelong* impact on the people in your sphere of influence.

Kids, your mom and I have tried to consistently teach you what we know, but the truth is we keep learning more than we did five, ten, or fifteen years ago. We keep wanting to teach you all about it, but at some point, you need to have a true, deep desire to learn on your own.

> *"An intelligent heart acquires knowledge, and the ear of the wise seeks knowledge." (Proverbs 18:15)*

In fact, that is the first point we wanted to share in this chapter: Your own desire to learn must be consistent, and you must know its worth.

You can't read one biography and think you know all about history.

You can't read one marketing book and think you know all about sales.

You can't do one Bible study and think you know all about the Bible.

You can't read one book on leadership and think you know all there is to know about being a leader.

Learning is not a box you check off. It's a lifestyle of being open to new insights, even in familiar areas, and letting your knowledge evolve.

Consistency over weeks, months, years, and decades is the key. Never stop reading; never stop learning. You might learn one thing in a five-hundred-page book, but that one thing might stay with you for the rest of your life. It could change the direction of a decision, a conversation, or a plan years down the road. If you had put the book down and watched TV or played games instead, you would have missed out on that life-changing knowledge.

No one has ever gotten ahead in life by only playing more video games, scrolling more social media, or being an expert on the ins and outs of a sitcom.

Get it in your head that you will be reading and learning until the day you die.

Another way to learn is to *listen* to those who have gone before you.

"My son, do not despise the Lord's discipline or be weary of his reproof, for the Lord reproves him whom he loves, as a father the son in whom he delights." (Proverbs 3:11–12)

I turned sixteen in February of 1987. The first day after I got my license, I eagerly got ready early and loaded up the family's baby blue 1971 Volkswagen Beetle, a car as old as I was with a stick shift and no seat belts.

It was a chilly, misty winter morning, and I couldn't have cared less! I was embarking on the first day of a lifetime of freedom. I eased out of the driveway and off I went. A half mile from home, I began the descent down a long, steep hill with a nearly ninety-degree curve at the bottom. I didn't care; I shifted my car up to fourth gear and started accelerating. I slammed on the brakes, but I was approaching the curve *way* too fast.

As the car slid out of control, I heard my dad's voice in my head: "Son, a Volkswagen's engine is in the back. That makes them back-heavy and more prone to flip on a sharp curve. Be careful."

I had to think fast. Unable to stop or turn, I steered the car straight through the curve into the front yard of a nice little home at the bottom of the hill.

Please don't hit the house, I prayed.

The house was straight ahead, coming up fast. At the last second, I swerved. With any luck, I'd come to a stop on the yard, and the tire tracks would be the only evidence of my mistake.

Little did I know it was a two-story house, and I had only been driving toward the top one. The moment I swerved, I hit the top side of a ten-foot retaining wall, unnoticed until it was too late.

I can still remember the noise of my tires hitting the bricks. I remember being airborne and seeing the lower driveway racing toward me. I remember the sudden stop when the nose of my now dearly departed VW Beetle hit the driveway and I lurched forward to kiss the windshield. I remember the millisecond of balancing on the front bumper before the car fell over on the driver's side. I can still hear all those terrible sounds to this day.

As I lay there on the door, I was certain I was dead.

Then I began to move and realized I wasn't dead after all. I wasn't even hurt! I reached up to crank down the window on the passenger side, pulled myself out, and walked home.

Several minutes later, my dad and I pulled into the house's upper driveway. My poor little car was lying in a pool of engine fluid, yet unnoticed by the owners of the house.

They arrived at the same time we did, having just dropped off their children at school.

Our neighbor, whom we had never met, said "Nice to meet you! So glad you dropped in!"

The mother, after looking over the scene, drew in a deep breath and exclaimed, "My petunias!" I can only assume the adults worked it all out; I couldn't stay for that conversation because I was late for school.

Later that afternoon, I heard the tow truck driver had said it was a good thing I was wearing a seat belt. The windshield was cracked where my head hit it, and according to him, I would have gone through it. I don't know if that's true, but I do know that the car I was driving did not have working seat belts.

My dad's words had helped me avoid the curve. God's protective hands had helped me survive the crash.

Now, decades after that accident, I still look figuratively over the wall, and I'm grateful for my dad's wisdom and warnings every time I'm headed for a "perilous curve." As a parent, I pray that even if you kids avoid a dangerous curve just to be thrown into another threatening situation, you can learn to trust our Heavenly Father the way I listened to and trusted my earthly father.

Learning from someone else is perhaps one of the greatest displays of wisdom. If you see what mistakes others have made, you can know how not to repeat those same mistakes.

> *"Intellectual growth should commence at birth and cease only at death." —Albert Einstein*

When your mother and I give you warnings about this or that, we are speaking from experience, including our own mistakes. We don't just share advice because we think we're better than you; we share it because we want to spare you the cost of learning the same lessons the hard way.

This is another reason that reading is so important. When you read accounts from the Bible or books on personal development, leadership, the military, and history, you get to see how other people have failed and succeeded. If you have the self-discipline to read about those lessons, apply them, and learn from them, you are way ahead of everyone else.

We were once leading a parenting conference, and we invited someone new to join us: a thirty-something pediatric nurse who had two children, ages six and eight. On learning that the conference was about parenting, she said, "I'm a pediatric nurse; I know all I need to know about kids and parenting."

That kind of confidence may sound impressive, but it actually shuts off the possibility of growth.

This is the same attitude described in Proverbs 16:18: "Pride goes before destruction, and a haughty spirit before a fall."

On the other hand, when your heart is open to instruction, willing to learn from anyone in any circumstance, your ability to succeed in anything increases exponentially!

It's shameful how a thimbleful of competence coupled with unchecked pride can shut you off from learning more.

This is one of the greatest frustrations for all parents—and it will be for you, too. Most instruction comes from parents. Sure, friends, teachers, and coaches have some influence, but not nearly as much.

Parents also have the most vested interest in their children's future success. So why were you so quick to dismiss our advice?

FROM MOM: Kids, the reason I wanted you to be with me in the kitchen was so you could learn. I wanted you all to learn by doing, and every time you weren't able or willing to, it hurt my heart a little because I knew we were both missing out. I was missing out on time with you, and you were missing out on learning more about meal prep, cooking, baking, and nutrition.

I didn't want to force you, like it was a chore. Lessons only truly land when you want to learn them.

On the flip side, I love it when you call me and ask for help. It gives me more time with you, and it makes me feel good to know you are still learning.

FROM DAD: I know that you all got tired of me telling you what to do. I probably felt more strongly about this than any other value. My parents were wise and willing to teach me anything I asked, and I wanted you to feel like you could have some kind of advantage if we gave you full access to our experiences and mistakes. That's why we talked so openly about them and helped you work through your problems.

As discussed in previous chapters, we set up our living room to be a laboratory of learning. Our desire was to create an environment where you learned almost by accident because we were available as often as possible, and we wanted to give you time to work through things.

We realize that we didn't always hear you out. We realize we didn't always give you the best advice. We even realize that we didn't always stay up with you to finish a conversation. We know that there were times we cut you off prematurely, which caused you to stop asking questions. But our hope was that in the long term, you would remain curious and teachable. Even in our imperfection, we wanted the culture of our home to be one of learning, listening, and openness to ideas.

We tried so often to not be jealous or miffed when you came home from some camp or party and started gushing about a world-changing philosophy you learned there—completely forgetting that we had been teaching you that same philosophy ad nauseam for years.

This happened so often that we decided to stop saying, "Hmmm, sounds familiar. I wonder where you might have heard that before...."

We chose to be happy that the values we taught you were being reinforced, no matter who got the credit. Letting go of the need for validation allowed us to focus on what actually mattered: your growth, your understanding, and your readiness to pass those values on.

> **WARNING:** *From an early age, your own kids will begin to be influenced by others besides you. You will have a choice to make. Sometimes, they will not hold to the same values you want to teach them. You can pluck them out of that environment and keep them "safe" (until it happens again) or you can spend more time with them, listening, reteaching, re-emphasizing, and holding fast to the faith that you simply cannot control every influence and that your own influence must be consistent. Your mom and I prayed often that your teachers and coaches would be high-quality people you could learn from and that our values would be*

reinforced when they had your attention. We could not have been happier. The coaches and teachers in your life were fantastic! Your kids may not have the same quality of influencers that you had, though, so be involved. Listen. Correct if necessary. Don't assume.

In truth, you did learn a lot from folks other than us, and we are grateful for those people. They reinforced values like hard work, achievement, respect, generosity, graciousness, integrity, teamwork, and dependability.

You learned these things from folks like Bob Faulhaber, Nick Crabtree, David Wright, Resa Roberts, Derrel Martin, Nicole Hackmann, Regina Pullin, Patrick Doyle, Allan Malone, Linda Evans, Davis Draper, Brandon Bottoms, Ben Prine, Joel Benson, Connie Bilbe, Katy Fagiolo, Megan Strawbridge, Kurt Snyder, Adam Pharris, Jonathan Casey, Megan Smith, Christi Mueller, Julie Groves, Dan and Michele Wilberscheid, Kelcey Tippitt Miller, Eric and Julia Dyer, Daniel and Samantha Allen.

These people modeled values we cherished, and they showed up when you needed them. That matters more than you know. We are so grateful that others were willing to teach and you were willing to learn.

Being teachable is one of the most sought-after qualities in a potential employee. Someone who is unteachable, too stubborn to learn from others, will quickly find themselves alone, desperate to know why no one cares about them. And that person will never fully understand that they must listen first and speak second.

> *"A fool takes no pleasure in understanding, but only in expressing his opinion."* *(Proverbs 18:2)*

How wise it would be if all kids listened to their parents and learned from their mistakes!

LIFETIME LEARNER CHECKLIST

- Are you always eager to learn more?
- Do you listen well to those who have life experience?
- Are you too prideful to learn from others?
- Never, ever stop learning.
- Be willing to be stretched in your learning. Become comfortable with being uncomfortable.

VALUES

The Value of Purpose

The Value of Respect

The Value of Diligence

The Value of Self-Discipline

The Value of Humility

The Value of Being a Lifetime Learner

The Value of Generosity

The Value of Marriage

The Value of Faith

The Value of Righteousness

The Value of Words

The Value of Love

The Value of Thinking for Yourself

The Value of Traditions

The Value of Hospitality

The Value of Purity

Chapter 10

BUSY IS NORMAL, IMPACT IS RARE

*"Someone's sitting in the shade today because
someone planted a tree a long time ago."*

—WARREN BUFFETT

*"A generous person will prosper; whoever
refreshes others will be refreshed."*

(PROVERBS 11:25, NIV)

THE VALUE OF GENEROSITY

I (Dad) know a man who was a very successful businessman in
his forties and fifties. Now in his late seventies, he has amassed
a great deal of wealth and is giving it away. He spends two
or three days a week researching charities and meets with me
often about the needs of the church we both attend. When I
speak to him, his joy is off the charts. He is always smiling,
always happy, always in a good mood. You might think he

is that way because he's rich, but he's actually joyful because he gives.

The Holy Bible is so full of wisdom, you could spend a lifetime studying it and not catch all there is to learn from this divinely inspired work. There is one verse I have heard all my life but that I've only come to appreciate because of this gentleman: "It is more blessed to give than to receive." (Acts 20:35)

How many people want to receive more than they want to give? Here's a hint: The gambling industry alone is worth literally billions of dollars.

And yet, my friend is not an anomaly. I have felt that pull to generosity, too. Perhaps not on his level, but in small things. When I take your car to fill up the tank, I feel good about that. There really is something to being generous, and we wanted you all to learn that feeling, too. But when it comes to generosity, giving away money is just scratching the surface.

GIVING SOMEONE YOUR TIME

Time is a very valuable resource. By setting up our living room the way we did, we wanted the four of you (and your friends) to feel like you had unlimited access to our time. Our desire was to be present, to "give away" as much of our time to you, your friends, and your pursuits as possible. And we hope you can do the same for your kids.

Of course, it is difficult to strike a balance between giving your time away and not letting others distract you from your own goals and dreams. But sometimes it's worth putting off work a little to share a coffee or a walk with friends.

Over the last several years, I have come to focus on a quote from noted speaker and author of one of my favorite books, *The Wealthy Gardener*, John Soforic: "Busy is normal, but impact is rare."

We have people in our lives who are always "on the go," flying around, never staying in one place. And they are proud that they are so busy. As I have reflected on this quote, I have begun to notice people who wear "busy" as a badge of honor. They never have quality time with anyone; they only divide up their time in tiny little pieces so that no one gets enough.

Max, you had a friend you would often invite to your house to play cards or watch an MMA fight, but he would never give you a straight answer. You would say, "You know how he is. He's so busy that he can't commit to hanging out with the guys, even with ten days' notice." This is *not* how you make an impact in the lives of others.

The point is, be careful, be smart, be deliberate, exercise discipline, and work on balance. But also be generous with your time. Not everyone will get your time, but when you do choose to give that away, give it wholeheartedly and happily. It will certainly make an impact.

LOANING OUT YOUR THINGS

A major part of a generous mindset is how you feel about "your stuff." Some people are very protective of their things, afraid they will get broken. It takes maturity to be willing to let someone borrow your car, your chainsaw, or your cake decorating kit.

Our neighbor, Phillip Baker, has many nice things. But he has never hesitated to lend anything to anyone. Better still, he will offer it to you before you even know you need it.

We were going to help Max move into his apartment in Louisville, Kentucky, and I had asked Phillip about borrowing his trailer. Not only did he loan it to us right away, he even insisted that we use his truck to pull it! That is generosity.

Anyone who knows your mom well knows that she has a soft spot in her heart for young mothers. (I guess that makes sense, since she was a young mother of four small children herself once.) When we moved to Cookeville, we purchased a house with an in-ground pool. Within a few years, Max, Levi, Emma, and Audrey were old enough to be responsible for other children.

At that point, Mom opened up the pool to young mommas and encouraged them to come relax while she and you kids helped keep an eye on their children. Over the years, our pool has become "the place" for moms and their little ones to come and play. One thing I've noticed about your mom is how she goes out of her way to convince other moms that we *want* them to come over. Mom has said that it brings her so much joy when a small child learns to swim in our pool.

When you loan out things that are valuable to you, you are living as if they don't really belong to you anyway. We think that is maybe the point. God owns it all, and we are only stewards.

GIVING SOMEONE YOUR TALENTS

You each have a set of skills, and you need to use those skills to make money so you can pay your bills and feed your family. But you can also use your talents and abilities to help others and make a generous impact.

It is a difficult thing to know when to put your services out there for profit and when to give them away. You will feel taken advantage of, and you will occasionally feel like you are wasting your time. You must show wisdom in how you choose to be generous with your special skills.

Max, it has always made us proud that, although you live three or four hours away, you will come back into town to help your old taekwondo instructor administer another black belt. You will spend the better part of a Saturday there and often have to take time off work. You aren't getting paid for that, but you are giving back to an organization that invested in you.

Hopefully, you all can find time in the future to help teach or coach a sport you love. Not everything is about making more money; sometimes it's more important to make an impact.

Levi, we know you have a calling to work with kids. Every year, you take time off work to volunteer Monday through Friday at our church's Vacation Bible School. That has always made us proud.

Emma, you are a world-class babysitter, and you have made lots of money doing that. But to a certain family we all love, you often offer your services for free so the parents can have a night out to themselves. You are making an impact.

Audrey, we have watched you struggle between satisfying your desire to sometimes be alone (a feeling we understand as outgoing introverts) and giving your time to your friends who want to hang out. So many times, we have watched you go to their house, meet them in town, invite them over, or chat with them on the phone when your inner self was begging you to be alone with your thoughts. You are making an impact, too.

Over the next few decades, all of you will acquire marketable skills that others will need. It will take wisdom, experience, trial and error, and learning from your own mistakes to figure out when to make an impact and when to make money. Both are worthwhile. Finding the balance is the hard part.

GIVING AWAY YOUR HARD-EARNED MONEY

We tried to exemplify generosity and charity as much as we could, while at the same time demonstrating frugality and wisdom. When you were younger, we had less money, so we squeezed what we could out of every dollar.

I mentioned in an earlier chapter how your mom would cut coupons and take all of you on long grocery trips to multiple stores every other Thursday to get the best deals. Every time we went out to eat, you were only allowed to drink water. We made you turn off the lights before you left a room, take shorter showers, and scrape the bottom of every jar of peanut butter and mayonnaise so none would go to waste.

FROM MOM: We couldn't be generous if we weren't smart. I believed it was my responsibility as the mom of the house to find little ways to save the family money. It's hard to be generous when you don't have anything. I wanted to teach you all that in order to be in a position to give, you need to make smart decisions about your spending. I know you've all heard me say, "Everybody gets water," or "You two can share a large fry," or "We can save money if we shred our own cheese rather than buying pre-shredded cheese." Save your money so you can give more of it away.

We remember multiple conversations with you about why we wanted you to be financially stable. We wanted to encourage you to be in a position to help others. In fact, we would probably say that the number one reason we wanted you to have jobs so early in life was so that you could sooner reach a point of being able to help fund mission trips and charities.

But this, too, requires wisdom. Levi, I remember when you were sixteen years old, you had been working for two full years and had a pretty nice sum in your bank account. Once you started driving, though, you often went out to eat with your friends. You told us about the time you went with five of your friends to grab a bite at Steak 'n Shake: You threw your debit card down on the table and said, "I got this." That was not wise. While we've always been proud of your generosity, we're thankful you're a little more discerning about your spending today.

We also expect that wherever you kids go in this world, you will be involved and financially invested in your local church. We expect you to give at minimum 10 percent of your income to that church, but also to go beyond that by offering your time and support however you can.

This is the beginning of generosity: giving consistently and happily as an act of worship.

Why is generosity an act of worship? We believe that God gives us the physical strength to do our jobs. We believe that He provides us with the brain power to think through our daily problems. We believe that He protects us from life-altering injuries so that we can earn a living. We believe that He provided you with your job. Therefore, we acknowledge that we could do nothing without Him. Being generous to His church is simply a first step in living a generous life. In our opinion, this act of worship should come first; before you give your hard-earned money to other people or causes, you must give it to God.

> *"Honor the Lord with your wealth and with the first fruits of all your produce; then your barns will be filled with plenty, and your vats will be bursting with wine." (Proverbs 3:9–10)*

Giving money to others comes after giving to your church.

Buying your friend a meal comes after giving to your church.

Donating to a charity comes after giving to your church.

Only those who attend your local church will support it. Even nonbelievers support charities. Support your local church first.

> *"One gives freely, yet grows all the richer; another withholds what he should give, and only suffers want." (Proverbs 11:24)*

GENEROSITY CHECKLIST

- Are you afraid to be taken advantage of?
- Do you manage your time wisely enough to be able to give any of it away?
- Do you look for ways to use your skills, talents, and abilities to bless others?
- The generous person always seems to have plenty.
- The stingy person always seems to be in need.

VALUES

The Value of Purpose

The Value of Respect

The Value of Diligence

The Value of Self-Discipline

The Value of Humility

The Value of Being a Lifetime Learner

The Value of Generosity

The Value of Marriage

The Value of Faith

The Value of Righteousness

The Value of Words

The Value of Love

The Value of Thinking for Yourself

The Value of Traditions

The Value of Hospitality

The Value of Purity

Chapter 11

LEAVING YOUR FATHER AND MOTHER

*"To get the full value of joy you must
have someone to divide it with."*

—MARK TWAIN

*"Marriage is the highest state of friendship.
If happy, it lessens our cares by dividing
them, at the same time that it doubles our
pleasures by mutual participation."*

—SAMUEL RICHARDSON

THE VALUE OF MARRIAGE

When asked how he still looks so good in his seventies, famous actor Don Johnson, who has been married to his wife since 1999—an eternity for a Hollywood celebrity—said, "Marry right. A bad marriage will age you."

One beautiful spring afternoon, Mom and I were gathered in our bedroom with all four of you kids. She was stretching her hamstrings after our morning hike, still glistening with a small amount of sweat. I remarked to you kids how lucky you are to have a mom who takes care of herself, who enjoys outdoor activities, and who doesn't mind hiking through woods, dirt, streams, and rocky terrain on a Saturday morning.

Audrey, in her sweet little eight-year-old voice, said, "Daddy, who do you love more, me or Momma?"

I replied, "Audrey, you know I love you very much, but it's not even close. I love your mom *way* more than I love you, and I hope that your future husband will say that about you, too!"

Maybe I was too harsh, but the point needed to be made then and hundreds of times thereafter: A marriage is the *preeminent* human relationship. That relationship deserves your best effort, your sharpest creativity, your deepest forgiveness, and your utmost loyalty.

I argue that while parenting is hard, marriage is harder. A bad or even mediocre marriage will make parenting (and everything else, frankly) much harder; but a wonderful marriage makes even the hardest parts of life a little bit easier.

Kids, we have been more deliberate in trying to model a good marriage than any other value I can think of. Our belief in the sanctity of marriage, especially the power of a good marriage, is unmatched by almost any of our other beliefs, values, or creeds.

We believe that a solid marriage creates many positive benefits. I have said many, many times that the greatest predictor of success for children is having grown up in a home with parents who loved each other deeply and openly.

The following are some of the benefits of a happy marriage.

SECURITY

We believe that when parents openly love each other, their kids will feel more secure about the world. The opposite is certainly true as well; kids who grow up in a home with parents who only coexist—parents who don't dote on each other, don't love spending time together, don't eat dinner together often, and don't go to bed at the same time—end up becoming a little insecure.

Children don't always have the vocabulary to describe what they feel, but they know when something is off. They feel it in the tension at the dinner table, in the silence in the car, and in the way their parents avoid eye contact. Even if no one ever says it out loud, kids can sense when love isn't thriving.

In my experience, when children come from a broken or unstable home, their insecurity is palpable. It's often an issue they will struggle to overcome for many years.

I have had the privilege of performing many weddings, and for each engagement, I require multiple sessions (five to ten hours' worth) of premarital counseling before I agree to officiate. As of writing this book, I have logged over five hundred hours of premarital counseling. At the beginning of my first counseling session with each couple, I ask an open-ended question: "What is your story?" I tell each individual to begin as far back as they want in their life story and include whatever details they like.

In *every single case* where a person's parents are divorced, that is the *very first* thing they mention.

"My parents divorced when I was five."

"After I started middle school, my mom and dad got a divorce."

"My dad left my mom before I was born."

"Right before my junior year of high school, my mom had an affair, and she and my dad got divorced."

One young man or woman after another, without being prompted, will *open* with this same story: "My parents are no longer together."

A mediocre marriage has a noticeable impact on the children in that family, and the impact of a nasty divorce leaves scars that may never fully heal.

For this reason alone, we consider marriage the single most important human relationship on earth.

CONFLICT RESOLUTION

A strong, healthy marriage is one in which conflict is handled in a mature way. When kids see their parents work things out in front of them, they learn how to face their own difficulties.

I know you all watched us work through several issues, and you saw us get mad at each other. I know you witnessed my frustration with you all and your mom, and you saw how I would sometimes exasperate your mom, too. I know there were times when I would scold you, but your momma would privately pull me aside and give me a different perspective, and I would come back to you and apologize or explain myself better.

This is conflict resolution in action. Your mom and I are on the same team, so we were never going to let you pit one of us against the other. We were determined to put up a unified front, so to speak, because we knew you outnumbered us.

This doesn't mean we never disagreed. We just chose to disagree respectfully and come to decisions together, as partners. That model taught you more than any lecture on communication ever could.

As future parents, you and your spouses need to be willing to resolve conflict in front of your kids, work things out in their presence, and let them hear you give your arguments for or against something. By doing this, you'll be giving your kids a leg up in life by allowing them to see how to handle difficult situations without resorting to yelling, personal attacks, or passive-aggressive behavior.

Of course, when we did disagree on how to discipline you all, we made those decisions in private. We didn't want you to figure out which of us was harsher and think the other would be easier to sway.

THE BEST MEDICINE

Another benefit to growing up in a home with loving parents is that the house is often filled with laughter.

As an often-quoted biblical proverb says, "A joyful heart is good medicine." (Proverbs 17:22)

We can't "scientifically" prove this, but we believe a happy home is a healthy home. None of you ever got too sick. We rarely went to the doctor for anything, and you almost never missed church, sports, or other events due to sickness. Did all our laughter as a family stave off illness for you kids? Your mom and I believe so.

A home in which there is tension—especially unresolved tension—is a breeding ground for stress-related sicknesses. It feels to us that kids from broken or unhappy homes have weaker immune systems because the environment in which they live is less healthy, less happy, and more stagnant.

Stress can show up in kids in subtle ways: frequent headaches, trouble sleeping, emotional outbursts, or a general sense of unease. A joyful home, by contrast, potentially gives kids a solid foundation for emotional and physical health.

If you want your kids to invite their friends to your house, create a joyful home that they'll *want* to bring their friends into. We wanted you to do your socializing at our house, so we tried to create a fun environment for that. But no amount of video games, trampolines, or dollhouses compensates for a tension-filled house.

These are just a few of the benefits of growing up in a home with loving parents. But how do you make that happen? How do you set up a marriage that will inspire your kids? What did we do to inspire you?

BEDTIME TOGETHER

I literally had no earthly idea that this one practice would make such a huge difference. I give all the credit to your mom. She insisted, from day one, that we go to bed at the same time. I liked going to bed at 9:00 p.m. She preferred midnight. So we compromised (sort of): We would both go to bed at 11:30 p.m.

We have stuck to this one routine for the entirety of our marriage, and it has been so healthy. Inconsistent bedtime routines were never an option.

Many husbands who suffer from pornography addiction admit that they get on their phones or computers *after* their wives go to bed. They stay up with an excuse like "I'm just not sleepy right now," or "I still have work to do," or "I'll come to bed in a little bit." Those are just excuses so they can be alone long enough to avoid getting caught looking at something they shouldn't. Going to bed at the same time as your spouse eliminates this possibility.

Many wives are self-proclaimed "night owls" who stay up to get more work done. They might clean the kitchen or pack tomorrow's lunches for their kids, then end up scrolling social media for hours as time slips away. This creates an unhealthy cycle of staying up late, getting up early with the kids, and being tired all day. It's better to get everything done before you both go to bed.

There are immature men who love to play video games after hours. That can become an addiction, too, making getting up for work a difficult morning ritual. He gets short and snippy with his wife in the morning because he stayed up too late playing games like a teenager. It's time to grow up.

There's something deeply symbolic about ending the day side by side. It reinforces that you are partners not only in parenting and decision-making, but also in rest and rhythm. That quiet time before sleep often becomes the space where the most honest, supportive conversations happen.

One of the best things to come out of this habit has been our ability to work through the issues of the day together. When you and your spouse lie there together in the quiet of the evening, you are able, for the first time all day, to talk without interruption. Your mind is clear as you talk about what happened that day, what decisions need to be made, and how to handle what might come next. This conversation has resulted in too many clear-minded decisions for your mom and me to count.

Of course, my real favorite part of going to bed at the same time as your mom is a subject you kids may not want me to talk about in detail. Suffice it to say, none of you would be here today if your parents didn't have a bedtime routine. Increased opportunity equals increased frequency. I'm just sayin'.

NO SLEEPING WITH US

Early on, we established two rules about our bed: We would protect our sleep, and we would protect our privacy. Setting strict rules about never letting you sleep with us protected our sleep and taught you how to manage yours. It was good for everyone, but it was so hard. We understood that you all wanted to crawl in bed with us. But we also knew one time would lead to many, and we believed from the beginning that we *must* prioritize our marriage while we loved and raised you to be outstanding members of society. That's why we protected our bed.

Parents who do not consistently sleep well and who are sexually frustrated due to lack of opportunity end up arguing a lot and becoming constantly grumpy. This is not a recipe for parenting success. We knew if we prioritized our relationship and provided you with a safe and secure homelife, you would sleep well. And it worked: All four of you slept great from day one, and we were all happier and healthier for it.

NO SITTING BETWEEN US

This rule was primarily for church, but we decided early on not to let you sit between us. This began when you were all old enough to fuss about who got to sit next to mom and who got to sit next to dad and who got to sit next to both of us at the same time.

We realized we could resolve this problem quickly if we decided, again, to prioritize our marriage. By not allowing any of you to sit between us, we were symbolically saying that we did not want anything or anyone to come between us. Our decision was validated as we saw other parents who obviously put their kids first beginning to struggle in their relationships and slowly starting to grow apart.

We would never suggest that we did everything right—not by a long shot—but we were aware of the stereotypes: the mom who makes her kids the center of her world, the dad who stays later and later at the office, the couple who drifts apart and gets divorced after their kids leave home.

That may sound dramatic, but it's common. And it doesn't happen all at once. It's a slow drift that begins with misplaced priorities and ends with two people who feel like strangers to each other, unable to enjoy what should have been the best season of their marriage. An act as simple as physically sitting together is a small signal that you're literally guarding your closeness.

THE INVESTMENT WITH THE GREATEST RETURN

When you were fifteen, thirteen, eleven, and nine, you kids were each given $1,000. We set up investment accounts and bought you each $1,000 worth of Apple Inc. stock. At the time, Apple was trading at $55 per share, and that value has since increased over 300 percent. Looking back, this was a great investment.

But that investment is a drop in the bucket compared to another investment your mom and I made: babysitting.

Yep, babysitting is *not* an expense; it's an investment that grows your relationship portfolio.

There is no amount of money (ask any divorce attorney) that's worth years of heartache, betrayal, and loneliness. We took advice from our older friends and immediately started scratching together enough money to pay a babysitter and go on dates at least every other week.

This may be the single most powerful decision we made for our marriage. When we moved to a new town, we began asking trusted people for recommendations for babysitters. We always had a first-, second-, and third-string babysitter on our call list. If you go out consistently, the money you invest in a babysitter is worth ten times as much in returns. You need time to yourselves, your kids need to learn to be away from you, and the babysitter needs the money. Win-win-win!

It's not just about getting a night out. It's about showing your kids that your relationship is worth prioritizing. Every time you leave for a date night, you're reinforcing the idea that a strong marriage doesn't happen by accident; it comes from intentional effort.

Trust me, your kids will be encouraged in the deepest parts of their soul when they see their parents getting dressed up to go bowling, to the movies, or out for a long walk.

And if that doesn't blow your helicopter parent socks off, here's another tip: Go on a weekend trip *without* your kids at least once a year!

Obviously, family vacations, weekend hikes, and ice cream stops should all include your kids. But you should be apart from your kids from time to time, and on at least one weekend a year, you should stay away overnight. This is time you need to work on your relationship, while you're alone together. The kids will be better for it, and so will your marriage.

Don't forget, your kids are always watching.

When your kids see that love means action—leaving the house, spending time together, investing money and energy into each other—they will begin to understand that marriage isn't background noise. It's the melody that helps everything else stay in tune.

WARNING: *At first, your kids will rebel. Do not be swayed. They will get over it. The first time you leave, your kids will cry and the babysitter will feel bad or even panic. Deal with it, but don't come home early unless someone is seriously hurt. If their crying successfully gets you to come home early, they will use that tactic again. Don't let your kids guilt you. They simply don't understand the long-term benefits yet. You are the adults; it's up to you to do the long-term thinking and trust that they will adapt. This adaptation phase will be hard, but don't be discouraged, and don't give in. Remember, whining gets you nothing.*

Your future spouse may or may not come from a home like ours. They may come from a broken or dysfunctional home. If this is the case, it is even more important that you prioritize your marriage. In our family, we value marriage so highly that few things surpass it on the list.

Is this your mindset? How do you feel about all of this? Truthfully, we don't know how you all felt about your mom and me going out and leaving you with April, Brianna, Summer, Julia, Courtney, or Ashley. We don't get the impression you've been holding a grudge, though!

Your mom and I have had many couples in our lives, including our own parents, whom we had the opportunity to watch and learn from. They truly showed us the way to live out a marriage that honors God while also being fun. Couples like John and Phyllis Weakley, Dick and Alvena Vaughn, and Buddy and Jo Neely have been happily married for over six decades! We also loved Jim and Margie Copeland; they were delightful to be around, as they loved Jesus so much, loved each other like newlyweds, and had fun all the time. They exemplified the meaning of "till death do us part." All these examples live in our hearts, and we seek to make an impact on others the same way these couples have impacted us.

For anyone else reading this book, you might think we are crazy. But let me tell you this: When a couple has young children over four years old and they say they have *never* been anywhere without the kids, that is *nothing* to brag about! Do not be proud of that fact. You are basically saying that you have not once prioritized the marriage relationship over the parenting relationship.

FROM MOM: My dad loved my mom. Your dad loves me. I wouldn't want to live any other way. But some people you meet will not have that experience. While that makes me sad, it also makes me determined to help you, if and when you get married, to have a wonderful, beautiful marriage. I want to help you with your kids so that you can continue to date each other. Please give me that chance.

MARRIAGE CHECKLIST

- Did you grow up in a home with parents who loved each other?

- Do you truly prioritize your spouse?

- Would your kids know how to treat their spouse well by emulating you?

- Be aggressively passionate about your marriage.

- Love is a verb.

VALUES

The Value of Purpose

The Value of Respect

The Value of Diligence

The Value of Self-Discipline

The Value of Humility

The Value of Being a Lifetime Learner

The Value of Generosity

The Value of Marriage

The Value of Faith

The Value of Righteousness

The Value of Words

The Value of Love

The Value of Thinking for Yourself

The Value of Traditions

The Value of Hospitality

The Value of Purity

Chapter 12

BELIEVING IS SEEING

"Be faithful in small things because it
is in them that your strength lies."

—MOTHER TERESA

THE VALUE OF FAITH

Only weeks after Max and Levi learned to ride their bicycles, they begged me to join them on a ride. Our neighborhood was very hilly and uneven, so as we climbed one hill and prepared for the first downhill coast, I started to tell the boys how careful we needed to be to avoid the obvious and not-so-obvious dangers on the road that could cause falls and wrecks.

Before I could get that out, though, Levi yelled, "Hey, Dad, watch this!"

He accelerated around a short curve and topped the biggest hill in the area. He then rode into the middle of the street, casually put his feet on the handlebars, and interlocked his hands behind his head!

As a dad, my heart nearly jumped out of my chest (I would have run over it). I wanted to scream at him to put his feet down, get both hands on the handlebars, and stop riding like he had a death wish.

But the words stopped in my throat. I only watched in horror as he rode his bike, hands-free, all the way to the bottom with no problem. Once the initial shock wore off, I started to reflect on my thoughts.

I realized Levi had clearly done this before. As if "Watch this!" weren't enough of a clue, his ability to coast like that without effort was the proof. He must have practiced.

I also realized that no matter how hard I tried, I would never be able to protect my kids all the time. I could warn them, forbid them from doing things, even ground them when they disobeyed, but that would only go so far.

Even the most well-meaning parental rules can't stop a child's natural curiosity, bravery, or independence.

The truth is, helicopter parenting is limited. The only "parental" protection we can always rely on is that of our Heavenly Father.

I rode my bike back home and told your mom what happened. At that point, we agreed we should pray even harder than we already did, asking our Creator, our Savior, to protect you all.

Honestly, we don't understand how people truly live life without faith. We love you kids so much that we wouldn't be able to sleep at night if we didn't have some measure of faith that God was protecting you. The love a parent has for their child is so deep that it feels like part of your heart is living outside your body. That vulnerability is terrifying.

That worry gets even worse when your kids start driving and dating. We want to feel in control, but we know we aren't.

When you become parents, you will feel this. It will either eat you alive or give you peace. In our opinion, parents who sleep with their small children, constantly track their every move, and scrub every surface down with bleach need to take a step back if they want their kids to grow and thrive.

WHAT IS "FAITH"?

The Bible defines faith like this:

> *"Now faith is the assurance of things hoped for, the conviction of things not seen." (Hebrews 11:1)*

The Merriam-Webster dictionary defines faith another way:

(1) allegiance to duty or a person; fidelity to one's promises

(2) belief and trust in and loyalty to God; firm belief in something for which there is no proof

(3) something that is believed especially with strong conviction

Why is faith a value that we want to teach you and hope you will raise your own kids with?

First, we believe that all of the values we've taught you come from a higher power and are all connected.

We believe all the values we hold dear come from our Maker, our Heavenly Father, God, the Creator of the universe. We have never seen Him, we have never audibly heard His voice, but we have faith that He exists and that He sees to all the order in our universe. We believe all the values we've taught come straight from God and are reinforced by His inspired Word, the Holy Bible. This is practicing faith. This is believing in what we cannot see and cannot prove exists.

We don't claim to have all the answers, but our lives have been shaped by this belief system. And when things don't make sense, this foundation gives us something to stand on.

The lives of our family and many of our friends tell a story of faith. Many of us practice what we preach, so to speak. Our faith is what keeps us moving forward in this world, swimming against a current that says to get what you can, whatever it takes. Faith leads us to choose delayed gratification, generosity, honesty, and compassion, even when those values seem inconvenient or unprofitable.

When I was in school, my life was consumed by athletics. It didn't matter what form they came in: I would watch Monday

Night Football, Saturday morning tennis, and baseball whenever it was on one of our three TV channels.

No other way to say it, I *loved* sports (and still do, even if not as much as I used to).

By sixth grade, I longed to compete in a sport. I had played on several sports teams by that time, and I had enough talent, size, speed, and agility to keep up with my classmates.

As the annual middle school field day approached, I took it as an opportunity to begin "training." I entered all the races I could qualify for—including the 400-yard dash.

Being a sixth grader, I had no clue how long four hundred yards actually was. (Had I known it was the length of four football fields, I probably wouldn't have signed up!)

I started training in the front yard, running back and forth in full view of my dad, who watched from the windows. Eventually, he got curious and came outside.

"What are you doing, son?"

"I'm training for the 400-yard dash," I said, "and I'm going to win!"

My dad then asked me to show him what I thought four hundred yards was.

Turns out, I was *way* off.

To my dad's credit, he didn't laugh at me. Instead, he gave me advice: "If you do exactly as I say, I promise you will win the race."

He explained that all the other boys would underestimate the distance, just as I had, so they would shoot out of the gate only to tire out halfway through the race. In order to win, then, I would have to jog for the first hundred yards or so before turning on the jets.

"Close to the halfway mark, run with all you've got," he said. "You'll be behind by then, but *don't* get discouraged. Trust me."

This made no sense to me at all. How could I win by starting *slow*? Surely that would cost me the whole race and ruin my reputation in sports forever! (Middle schoolers are dramatic like that.)

On race day, I had a difficult choice to make: Should I trust my own instincts or my dad's advice?

Luckily, even at that age, I knew my dad was trustworthy, honest, caring, and smart.

Dad has never let me down before, I thought, *so even if I don't understand his advice, I'm going to trust him.*

Guess what: my dad was right. I won that race by at least twenty yards and went on to earn a reputation as the fastest kid in school! And all because I had faith in someone who knew better than me.

I learned a valuable lesson that day. That was the pivotal moment when I began to understand the true meaning of the word "faith."

Am I being a leader/father/husband/friend who people will blindly trust?

Do I trust my Heavenly Father the same way when He asks me to do something I don't fully understand?

Do my kids trust me so much that they will always follow my suggestions?

Parents, are you living a trustworthy life?

Business leaders, are you leading with enough integrity to earn your employees' trust?

We wanted to teach you kids that God is worth trusting. But there's another reason we wanted to teach you about faith. Ask yourselves this: When life gets difficult, do you truly believe that everything will work out for the best?

It's one thing to believe that God created the world. It's another to trust that He loves you enough to care about your personal struggles and help you overcome them.

A GIANT LEAP OF FAITH

Your mom and I went through a major test of faith in our sixth year of marriage.

Living together took some getting used to. We weren't quite ready for it. We struggled. We fought. We made bad decisions. We ate way too much and stayed up way too late. We were sharing one life. Yet big responsibilities were nowhere in our minds.

Then, six years into our marriage, we found out we were expecting our first child. Our thoughts were flooded with joy and fear, terror and elation, cute clothes and college funds. Suddenly, we couldn't make selfish, short-term choices anymore. A painful change was in order.

We went through doctor visits, hand-me-downs, name-choosing, the whole experience. And we grew up a little, too. We weren't "ready" (no one ever really is), but we were getting closer.

Then came August 11, 1999. About five weeks before our baby boy was due, your mom felt uneasy. She had grown accustomed to feeling the kicks and twists inside her belly, and she hadn't felt them in a day or so. We made an unplanned trip to the doctor's office, where they put her on a heart monitor. Time passed. Different nurses entered and exited with few words. Tension grew. Finally, a doctor we had never met entered the room, did a few more tests, and very plainly gave us terrifying advice:

"Your baby stands a better chance of surviving outside the womb than inside. We need to do an emergency C-section right now. Go straight to the hospital; they will be waiting for you."

Words cannot describe the intensity of our fear as we drove straight to the hospital.

Exactly like a scene from a medical drama, the ER nurses were indeed waiting for us. A whole team surrounded Mom, put her on a gurney, gave her anesthesia, and performed an emergency C-section in five minutes flat, an experience I have since come to refer to as "the quick gas and gut."

Afterward, Mom was recovering in the operating room. The blinds to the nursery were open, and I was told I could view our son through the window until he was ready for me to hold him. But the nurses closed the blinds. By then, the waiting room had started to pile up with supportive friends , like Kelly Hammer, who had been at home preparing food for a shower in our honor, who were helping to distract me from the horrible situation. I am grateful for all those who came to support me, I remember specifically Kelly since she was also pregnant with her and Chris's first child, due practically on the same day as Max was.

I DIDN'T KNOW THE HOSPITAL HAD ONE OF "THOSE" ROOMS

Shortly after the nurses closed the blinds, I was taken to a room that I didn't know existed. I would later call it "the bad news room." It's a room designed for maximum privacy, located away from the throngs of happy people waiting to catch a glimpse of their newest family member.

"Hi, Mr. Bailey," said a doctor I'd never met before. "My name is Dr. Toffaletto, and I'm the pediatrician on call. I am attempting to take care of your son. Mr. Bailey, your son has made no effort to move, breathe on his own, or even open his eyes. We have a breathing tube down his throat, but as of this moment, he has made no effort to live.

"We are doing everything we can, but we don't even know what's wrong with him, and therefore we don't know how to treat him. It doesn't look good, Mr. Bailey. We have called Children's Hospital to come and get him, but it will take them at least an hour to get here, and to be honest, I am not sure your son has that much time."

With that, he walked out.

Many of the events of that day are a blur. But I do remember that at some point, I was with our pastor, one of the greatest men I have ever known, Dr. Randy Davis.

He didn't know what to say. I didn't know what to say. For a brief moment, I wondered what it would cost to bury a child. I imagined a headstone with a single date on it for birth and death. I thought about where we would bury him, if it should be my hometown, my wife's, or here.

Clearly, I was sinking fast.

Brother Randy will never truly know how much his words helped me that day, as they snapped me out of my downward spiral: "Lee, you will need to make a decision very soon about whether you will stay with JoAnne or go with the ambulance to Children's Hospital. This is your most immediate decision. You don't need to think about anything beyond that."

Five minutes later, Dr. Toffaletto came back to say that an entire team of doctors and nurses from Children's Hospital had just arrived and were now treating our son.

We later found out that they had been called to help another baby in distress at a hospital across the street, but that baby had stabilized before they even arrived. They were already there when the doctor called!

By this time, Mom was regaining consciousness, and the neonatal intensive care physician entered our room to give an update. He knew what was wrong, but it still might be too late. Our son had lost most of his blood in the womb through a faulty valve in the umbilical cord, and when he was delivered, he had less than twenty percent of the blood volume needed to survive. His organs, including his brain, were most likely starved for blood and oxygen.

Medical professionals will already know this, but when babies are born, they are put through several tests and given what's called an Apgar score. Our baby's score was zero. He would have to be given multiple blood transfusions over the next twelve hours if we hoped for him to have any chance of survival.

Your grandmother had arrived to support your mom, so I chose to go to Children's Hospital with our baby. I remember very little about that time in the waiting room. People who heard about our situation were kind enough to come by the waiting room and give me encouragement. Occasionally, a nurse or doctor would come in with an update. Most of these updates were not good.

As the afternoon turned into night, the waiting room began to empty out. Eventually, the nurses told me that visiting hours were up and I couldn't see my son until tomorrow. The last person with me that day was a long-time friend, Travis Dunlap. We walked out to the parking lot to look for my car (someone else had driven it to the hospital and I had no idea where it was). Once we found it, he gave me a hug and walked away.

Alone, hungry, tired, scared, and emotionally spent, I finally took in a deep breath. Standing at the front bumper of my car, I spoke these words out loud: "Lord, JoAnne and I have been praying for months for a son who will one day further Your kingdom. How can his death accomplish that?"

Suddenly, my mind was flooded with memories of times when God was *faithful*, even in the midst of tragedy, like my birth mother's untimely death when I was only four years old. God reminded me that He gave His only Son to redeem a sinful and broken world. In that moment, helpless and alone, I said, "Lord, You are in control. You, and only You, can say how this is going to end. I trust You."

I stood in that dimly lit parking lot and physically raised my hands heavenward, as if I was holding my little premature son, symbolically giving him to God. "He is Yours," I whispered.

The world would have us believe that religion is a crutch, an artificial way to cope with life.

But all I can say is that the Bible is clear: The Holy Spirit will give us a "peace that surpasses all understanding." In the moment I felt most alone, I trustingly "gave up" what wasn't really mine to begin with. God entrusts us with children, but in the end, they are His.

The instant I raised my hands in that gesture, I felt a *peace* wash over me like never before. I understood then God cared about me and was going to comfort me and my wife—**regardless of what happened. And that was all I needed to know.**

If God showed us up front everything we would have to deal with in life, we couldn't handle it. Life is too full of inevitable pain and heartache. But God's grace is always enough for the moment we are in. That is all we need. I experienced a peace that no one can possibly explain, not even myself. I only knew I finally had enough peace, grace, hope, and faith to have a restful and rejuvenating night of sleep.

Though we would never wish it on you, your mom and I know you will definitely deal with pain, disappointment, and suffering—sometimes physical, sometimes emotional, and sometimes spiritual. Bad things will happen to you. People that you love will hurt you. Sometimes, you might even feel like God has abandoned you. But faith—believing what you cannot feel, holding on to what you cannot prove—will lead to growth, wisdom, and depth that few people have.

Your mom and I both put our faith in God that day. And how did that turn out? Well, you're still here, Max.

FROM MOM: In my very young and inexperienced heart, I could not believe or accept what was happening during those very real moments before and after the emergency C-section. I was so glad your dad was there with me, but in my insecure about-to-be-a-new-mom brain, I felt alone, scared, guilty. I felt like I had done something wrong, like somehow, this was my fault. It was only when the neonatal nurse took my hand and explained to me that there was nothing I could have done to prevent this that I was finally able to rest.

For me, that conversation with the nurse was one of the most pivotal moments in that entire experience.

I remember vividly the peace I felt afterward, a peace that could only come from God. Our faith, our family, and our church friends carried us through that time. I have said this before, but I just do not know how people go through trauma without the support of a church family. This experience strengthened and grew my faith like never before.

I remember feeling strongly that God was telling me to go to Rwanda on a mission trip. I believe that God gave me the spiritual gift of hospitality, and I feel I am most in His will when I use it. I have no memories in my life of not knowing God was there. When I was a teenager, I did not pursue discipleship and prayer like I should have. I didn't work very hard to learn how to pray or study my Bible. It wasn't until college and the early years of marriage that I started taking more responsibility for my relationship with God. Max's birth helped me see faith in action.

My own discipleship was still sporadic, but I studied the Bible, I prayed, and I grew in my relationship with Christ. While I still have much to learn, I know that He has saved me not only from an eternity in hell but also from a life of heartache and pain. While I may have sometimes needed forgiveness, I have never wanted for faith.

FAITH CHECKLIST

- Do you struggle with letting go and trusting God?
- Are you afraid of something that hasn't happened yet?
- Do you stay awake at night worrying?
- God is in control. Believe that, and live by it.
- Your faith blesses others.

VALUES

The Value of Purpose

The Value of Respect

The Value of Diligence

The Value of Self-Discipline

The Value of Humility

The Value of Being a Lifetime Learner

The Value of Generosity

The Value of Marriage

The Value of Faith

The Value of Righteousness

The Value of Words

The Value of Love

The Value of Thinking for Yourself

The Value of Traditions

The Value of Hospitality

The Value of Purity

Chapter 13

DOES THE END ALWAYS
JUSTIFY THE MEANS?

*"To see what is right and not do
it is the worst cowardice."*

—CONFUCIUS

*"Character is doing the right thing
when nobody's looking."*

—J.C. WATTS JR.

*"A good name is to be chosen rather than great
riches, and favor is better than silver or gold."*

(PROVERBS 22:1)

THE VALUE OF RIGHTEOUSNESS

One day, we were driving our Toyota Corolla down a Tennessee highway when someone pulled out in front of us, causing a wreck that totaled the vehicle.

That Corolla had a long history. We had gone to the Toyota dealership just eighteen months before the accident, having decided (against *all* advice) that we needed a new car. After test-driving several cars, we settled on a shiny Toyota Corolla with only fifteen miles on the odometer.

The problem was that we couldn't afford it, not by a long shot. The salesman told us that. The general manager told us that. My old college roommate's dad, who worked as a mechanic at that dealership, told us that. But we were undeterred, even after all these people had dared to tell us the truth! We hung around and kept asking questions, until finally we were allowed to lease the car for one year.

After one year, we had to turn it in or buy it for more than the original sticker price. We also couldn't put more than 12,000 miles on that car within those twelve months. But we were there to buy a car for me (Dad) because I was commuting around 150 miles a day to and from work. We both knew we would already hit that limit in the first three months.

Sure enough, by the time our one-year term was up, we had already put about 80,000 miles on it. We were so upside down on that car, I had to crawl on my hands and knees to my own employer, American Fidelity Bank, and ask my boss to give me a loan much higher than the car was worth. Reluctantly, my boss approved the loan, and we began making even higher payments on a car now worth about forty percent less than when we bought it.

At the same time, we were going through a study at church on financial management produced by Crown Financial Ministries. We started to understand that we were in this bad spot financially due to our own mismanagement. We took the advice of our counselors and begin paying off our debt with every single extra dollar we could scrape together. We sold some belongings and started eating at home more often. Over the next six months, we paid down the debt significantly, but we still owed a *lot* more than the car was worth; I recall correctly, we owed around $8,000 while the car was worth around $4,000 when the accident occurred.

Even though the wreck was not my fault (as everyone, including the other driver and their insurance company, agreed), we still had to pay off the loan to my employer for a car we couldn't even drive anymore.

I started losing sleep over this debt. The more I dwelt on it, the angrier I felt. After a traffic accident that was entirely someone else's fault, I was without a vehicle *and* in the hole for $4,000. This was plain unfair.

The more I told the story, the more people sided with me. I was gaining all kinds of support for our unfair situation. Then someone made the suggestion that I start having "neck pain" and "back pain." Those symptoms are hard to pinpoint, but since I had not been to a doctor before the accident, I could theoretically use that excuse to get the insurance company to pay me more.

I'm not going to lie: I considered it. At that time in our marriage, $4,000 might as well have been $400,000. It was a huge amount to pay off in debt alone and still need to replace our car. I began to work through in my head how to tell the story of my back pain and neck pain. I knew I needed to be convincing, that this could make or break my case for a bigger payout.

It's not easy for me to share how evil and dark my heart can be sometimes. I was fully prepared to engage in insurance fraud, to give up my integrity, for only $4,000. Imagine if I had needed more money, right?

Just as I was considering this option, we got to the lesson in our Crown Financial Ministries study about total honesty at work. This lesson was about having so much integrity that you refuse to steal even a paper clip—the type of integrity that stands out and that God rewards. As if this study hadn't already made a big enough impact on us, now I was figuratively cowering in the corner, full of conviction.

Finally, I decided that being honest was the only way I could continue to look myself in the mirror. The next day was Monday morning, and I had not yet heard from the insurance company on a final offer. So, as I drove into work, I prayed to the Lord to repent; I told Him how I had taken time out of my employer's work day to complain and scheme and so forth, and how my anxiety was keeping me from doing my job with excellence.

I decided to go to work with the right attitude this time. No matter what happened, we were going to act with integrity, to "do the right thing." Even though we had stupidly put ourselves into this predicament, we were also working ourselves out of it. We would accept any offer that seemed fair based on the Kelley Blue Book value of our car.

I put the car situation out of my mind and focused on my work. I would no longer lose productive company time wringing my hands over this deal. God was in control, and I had to accept that.

Later that week, I got a call from the other driver's insurance company:

"Mr. Bailey, this is Janice from Progressive Insurance. We finally got an adjuster to look at your car, and we believe that $12,000 is a fair offer."

I was *floored*.

I knew the Kelley Blue Book value on the car was only $4,000. I also knew that all insurance companies use the same tools to value cars. So where did they get that huge number?

"Mr. Bailey, do you accept our offer?"

"Yes, of course," the words tumbled out. "But ... I'm a little confused. Do you mind telling me how you reached that offer?"

"Well, your car is eighteen months old, and it only has four thousand miles on it."

I knew this wasn't true; by the time of the accident, the car had well over 100,000 miles on it. Now I was faced with another dilemma.

Why did I ask a follow-up question? I thought. *Why didn't I just take the offer and hang up? Now what do I do?*

It would have been so easy to take the offer and not have to worry about the loan anymore … but I had already committed to doing the right thing. It was the only way I would be able to live with myself.

I took a deep breath. "Ma'am, I have to be honest: The adjuster made a mistake. That car had a *hundred* and four thousand miles on it. As grateful as I am, I'm afraid your offer is too high."

Silence.

More silence.

I started to sweat, already imagining how much longer I'd be paying off that loan.

Finally, the insurance agent cleared her throat. "Mr. Bailey, once we extend an offer, company policy says we cannot retract it. Our offer stands at $12,000."

I couldn't believe it. Once everything was settled, we paid off the loan and used the rest of the money to buy a used Mazda

B2200, a beat-up two-door pickup truck. And just like that, we were out of car debt.

When I tell this story, I *never* want to imply that doing the right thing will always end in your favor. It often won't, at least not in the short term. As I was writing this chapter, Max told us he was in a car accident in Kentucky and he told the claim agent the truth, that he was delivering a DoorDash order, a confession that disqualified his insurance claim and cost him over $7,000.

He could have lied that he had already delivered the food. He could have not mentioned DoorDash at all. Telling the truth did cost him, but only money. **It didn't cost him his** *integrity.*

These are the choices that reveal true character: when the consequences for doing the right thing are steep, but you do it anyway. It's painful, but it's also powerful.

What it boils down to is this: Do you believe that you should do what is "right" even if it does not benefit you?

We wanted you kids to believe that. We believe it. But do we act like it? We have faith that God will take care of us, but do our actions show that?

The book of Proverbs is full of examples of this type of behavior, so it seems fitting to let the Bible do some teaching on this subject of righteousness:

> *"Such are the ways of everyone who is greedy for unjust gain; it takes away the life of its possessors." (Proverbs 1:19)*

Sometimes, greedy people win at first. But in the end, the honest prevail.

In Proverbs 2:7–13, the Bible describes God as a "shield" to those who walk in their integrity. God protects those who choose to live a life of high character:

> *"[He] stores up sound wisdom for the upright; he is a shield to those who walk in integrity, guarding the paths of justice and watching over the way of his saints. Then you will understand righteousness and justice and equity, every good path; for wisdom will come into your heart, and knowledge will be pleasant to your soul; discretion will watch over you, understanding will guard you, delivering you from the way of evil, from men of perverted speech, who forsake the paths of uprightness to walk in the ways of darkness."*

In Proverbs 3:7–8, we see the promise that character and integrity will bring healing to your flesh and refreshment to your bones. The idea here is that if you continue down a path of being dishonest, eventually you will rot from the inside out:

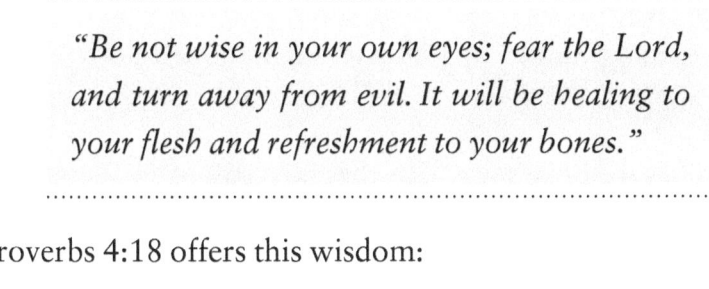

"Be not wise in your own eyes; fear the Lord, and turn away from evil. It will be healing to your flesh and refreshment to your bones."

Proverbs 4:18 offers this wisdom:

"...the path of the righteous is like the light of dawn, which shines brighter and brighter until full day."

There is so much to be said about this verse, but what I sense is that if you live a life—not a day or a week, but a life—of integrity, your path will shine. In other words, you will have clarity and purpose in your life. What you do will be noticed, and your efforts will be blessed.

As quoted from J.C. Watts Jr. in the beginning of this chapter, "Character is doing the right thing when nobody's looking." The Bible makes this point in Proverbs 5:21, which says that "a man's ways are before the eyes of the Lord."

You may think no one notices when you quietly do the right thing, but God does. And often others do, too, even if they never say a word.

Regret is an emotion often associated with doing the wrong thing. I do not believe that anyone ever regrets doing the right thing, even if there is no immediate benefit. Proverbs 10:22 promises that the righteous will be blessed *and* no sorrow will be added to the blessing! This is a great promise I see lived out time and time again. Doing the right thing leads to a clear conscience.

What does the Bible say will be the end result of doing the right thing over a lifetime?

> *"Whoever pursues righteousness and kindness will find **life**, **righteousness**, and **honor**."* (Proverbs 21:21)

The pursuit of righteousness is different than doing what is right once. It is a lifetime of caring more about your character than the short-term benefits of dishonesty. As you pursue righteousness, here's what you will find:

Life – How big is this word? Finding "life" means finding fulfillment. It means finding purpose, joy, and success. Finding "life" is finding meaning. Isn't this what everyone wants? You get that by pursuing righteousness.

Righteousness – If you pursue righteousness, you will find righteousness. What does that mean from a practical standpoint? Maybe it means that over time, as you do the right thing, the right thing will be done to you. Maybe it means that you will experience all the benefits that the Bible promises (too many to list here) of someone who is righteous. Maybe it means that you will also find like-minded people, family, friends, and coworkers who also pursue righteousness, and an atmosphere of great trust will settle over your family and colleagues.

Honor – If you pursue righteousness over a lifetime, you will find honor. Proverbs 10:7 promises that the someone who has a reputation of always doing the right thing will be fondly remembered. This word is layered with legacy.

Our church has a music school, and one of the instructors is a guy named Jimmy Bilbrey. He is one of the most talented musicians I have ever known. He teaches students violin, guitar, piano, banjo, mandolin, and likely several other instruments. He is kind and thoughtful. He is not a member of our church, but he is involved in a church about five miles down the road. He has the largest student load of any of the instructors at our school. His schedule is always full; he even has a waiting list!

Why do I mention him in this chapter?

Whenever he has a break in his schedule, Jimmy walks outside and picks up trash. I have witnessed him do this dozens of times, and I can only assume he's done it hundreds of times. He doesn't do it for credit or community service. He does it to be kind.

Jimmy does the right thing even when no one is watching. It's in his character. It's who he is. His life is defined by the pursuit of righteousness, and walking around our property to pick up trash is an outward expression of inner integrity.

FROM MOM: I would say that this is the main value I wanted you to learn in our house: doing the right thing. Be honest. Be kind. Show love. Be patient. Do the right thing for the right reason. Teaching values is so much harder than teaching behaviors.

RIGHTEOUSNESS CHECKLIST

- Where are you lacking in the area of righteousness?
- Have you already decided, before you're tested, that you will do the right thing?
- Do you believe that doing the right thing will eventually work in your favor?
- As Dumbledore once said, "We must all face the choice between what is right and what is easy."
- Righteousness is a lifelong pursuit.

e whi...
did not of which
...id I do done, you mus...
...id I do, have you real feeling of this mo...
...my real feeling commence
...ds you my approache...
to offer. Caroline I am
...ears from perceived not su...
...that I have nervous are
Caroline moment love
Caroline My dearest Ca...
...off tea...

VALUES

The Value of Purpose

The Value of Respect

The Value of Diligence

The Value of Self-Discipline

The Value of Humility

The Value of Being a Lifetime Learner

The Value of Generosity

The Value of Marriage

The Value of Faith

The Value of Righteousness

The Value of Words

The Value of Love

The Value of Thinking for Yourself

The Value of Traditions

The Value of Hospitality

The Value of Purity

Chapter 14

DEATH AND LIFE ARE IN THE POWER OF THE TONGUE

"The biggest communication problem is we do not listen to understand. We listen to reply."

—STEPHEN COVEY

THE VALUE OF WORDS

We had a side lot in our yard where we played football, volleyball, soccer, lacrosse, and even had a trampoline. The lot was near a busy road, and across that road was a house where two people lived. We would often wave to them, but even after living in that house for ten years, we had never officially met them.

One day, after Emma had graduated from high school and gotten a lacrosse scholarship at Lee University in Cleveland, Tennessee, I felt it might be time for a change. So one Saturday afternoon, when everyone else was gone, I walked to that big lot where Emma's soccer and lacrosse goals were still set up.

I was deep in thought as I slowly disassembled those goals and put them away, perhaps for good. Then suddenly, I was startled by a voice behind me.

"Well, it's the end of an era."

I turned. It was the gentleman who lived in the house across the street.

"Hi, I'm Matt," he said. "My living room faces this part of your yard. I feel so bad that we've never officially met, even though we've passed each other for years. When I saw you taking down these goals, I just had to come over."

"So nice to finally meet you, Matt!" I shook his hand. "I'm Lee. I'm so glad you came to introduce yourself."

"Well, I needed to tell you something: We've been watching your daughter for years. Day in and day out, morning to night, she'd be training in the snow, in the rain, in the heat. I just had to tell you that whatever she accomplishes in her life, she's earned it. She is such an inspiration."

This is still one of my all-time favorite conversations I've had about my kids. I could have shared this story sooner when talking about diligence, self-control, or even humility. But it felt most fitting to share here, in the chapter on the power of the tongue.

Words really do have the power to make someone's day, week, or even year. They also have the power to kill someone's dreams and hurt someone for a lifetime.

The Bible tells us that both death and life are in the power of the tongue. In this chapter, we wanted to cover four aspects regarding this value.

The first is that you can use words to lift someone up. The second is that you can choose to pass up an opportunity for life-giving words of affirmation.

SPEAKING WORDS OF LIFE

> *"The mouth of the righteous is a fountain of life..." (Proverbs 10:11)*

You may not be naturally good at giving compliments. But when you notice someone has lost weight or played hard or done a good job on a presentation, yet you choose not to say anything, you have missed an opportunity to bless someone.

This is why we do not let any of you kids use being "shy" as an excuse to not look someone in the eye and say "Hello," or "Thank you," or "Could you please tell me where the nearest restroom is?"

Using words to speak life is an important life skill, and it doesn't matter if you are naturally good at it or not. Some of you do not naturally use words expressively, and therefore you feel awkward when you try. Try anyway. Expressing appreciation or encouragement doesn't require a special occasion or a deep relationship; it only requires intention.

Imagine how much easier it would have been for Matt to stay in his living room and never walk across the street to tell me what he did. That would have been the easy thing. But he knew it would make a huge impact in my life, so he made that effort anyway. And now I'm telling that story here! Do not waste an opportunity to say positive things to people.

On the flip side, you can use words to tear people down—or you can have the self-discipline to hold your tongue.

As your mom and I raised you, we tried to create an environment where you would either (1) say the right thing, and it would be a blessing; or (2) *not* say the right thing, and it would feel like a curse.

Saying the right thing, as in Matt's example, is the "life" part of the power of our words. One of my favorite Scripture verses on this subject is Proverbs 25:11: "A word fitly spoken is like apples of gold in a setting of silver." This basically means that your ability to speak wise words at the right moment to a person who needs them is like a beautiful work of art.

Our neighbor said those nice words to me, and they were a blessing.

How sad it is to think something nice, knowing it would make someone feel good, and yet choose not to say it!

Have you ever thought to yourself how nice someone's hair or clothes look? Do you tell your friends how much you appreciate them? Kind words are doorways to meaningful conversations. Choose to open them.

NEGLECTING TO SPEAK WORDS OF LIFE

I (Dad) was very active in the Fellowship of Christian Athletes (FCA) in high school. I was even voted president of my FCA high school chapter for three years. I always wore Christian-themed T-shirts and would almost daily wear little buttons that said things like "God loves you," or "Jesus is the reason for the season." Anyone who saw me knew I was a Christian.

There was also a girl in my high school who had a bit of a bad reputation; she was disruptive and rude to the teachers, and she was often sent home due to dress code violations. I didn't know her personally—I don't even remember her name—but I had seen her around, and I knew she wasn't the kind of person I would normally be friends with.

One day, that girl approached me at my locker and asked, "Do you really believe all those things you say you stand for?"

Looking back now, I realize what a brave act that was. I'm sure it took guts for her to walk up to a guy who might judge her, given how different our lives were. I'm sure it wasn't easy to ask such a heavy question to a classmate who was practically a stranger. Maybe she had even tried to approach me a few times before but chickened out.

I should have seen the opportunity in front of me, the small window that had opened. Instead, I looked her straight in the eye, said, "Yes, I do," and walked away without another word.

To my memory, we never spoke again throughout the rest of our high school days, and I have not seen her since graduation. The window was closed.

Apparently, that girl was lost and had been seeking answers for a while, to no avail. I had a chance to share some life-changing words that might have finally given her a path forward. But I didn't take it. I held my tongue at the wrong time.

Death and life are *both* in the power of the tongue. I did not choose to share life, and by holding my tongue, I invited death to find someone who wanted to be rescued.

Do not pass up an opportunity to share a good word, or you will regret it later, possibly even for the rest of your life.

Of course, the other side of this coin is that you can truly hurt someone forever with your words.

SPEAKING WORDS OF DEATH

Yes, words can crush someone's spirit. The old adage "Sticks and stones may break my bones, but words will never hurt me" is a deep, sick lie.

A more accurate saying would be "Sticks and stones may break my bones, but words can *kill* me."

Instead of believing lies about sticks and stones, we encourage you kids to live by these words: "If you don't have anything nice to say about someone, don't say anything at all."

One thing we have worked on for years—to limited effect, it seems—is teaching you all to keep your mouth shut when your words are daggers. Of course, foolish man that I can be sometimes, I'm sure you learned some of this bad behavior from me in the first place.

Multiple times, we, as a family, have been in our living room talking about someone. I have spoken poorly about some of those people, including some of your friends.

Audrey, your heart hurts when I do that. I see it in your eyes. Your spirit is grieved when I say anything negative about anyone (even if it's true). I love that about you. You embody the value laid out in this chapter better than all the rest of your siblings. I am so sorry that at times, even though I preach the opposite, I am guilty of speaking death. I may not say bad things to people's faces, but that doesn't make it one iota better. I need to show more discipline in keeping those "death" words out of my mouth. Thank you, Audrey, for showing me my own inconsistencies.

> "Keep your mouth free of perversity; keep corrupt talk far from your lips." (Proverbs 4:24 NIV)

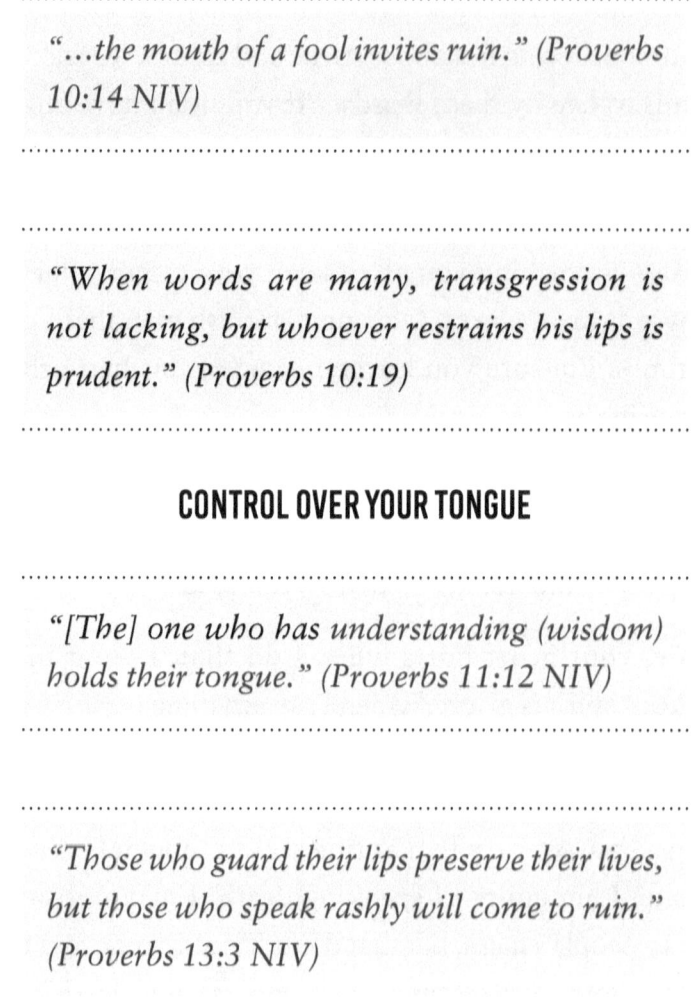

> *"...the mouth of a fool invites ruin." (Proverbs 10:14 NIV)*

> *"When words are many, transgression is not lacking, but whoever restrains his lips is prudent." (Proverbs 10:19)*

CONTROL OVER YOUR TONGUE

> *"[The] one who has understanding (wisdom) holds their tongue." (Proverbs 11:12 NIV)*

> *"Those who guard their lips preserve their lives, but those who speak rashly will come to ruin." (Proverbs 13:3 NIV)*

Of the four aspects of this value, the hardest to master is holding your tongue. It's difficult to swallow the words that so desperately want to come spilling out of your mouth, to have the self-discipline to listen intently without interrupting.

Stephen Covey, in his landmark book *The Seven Habits of Highly Successful People*, puts it this way: "Seek first to understand, then to be understood."

The self-control and self-discipline it takes to ready your ears and not your mouth is great indeed. In a world where constant communication is the norm, it is easy to believe that silence equals weakness. But in truth, restraint often shows greater strength than speaking.

Listening, ironically, is a key element of the power of the tongue.

But it's not the only element. Choosing to hold your tongue when you want to say something derogatory or disparaging is a major part of this principle.

Once again, Audrey, you are really great at this. You rarely, if ever, say anything bad about anyone. You don't agree when someone is speaking badly about someone else, even nonverbally. We can all learn from the way you handle such situations.

When you all are raising your own kids, you will deal with all four aspects of this very important virtue. You will want to teach them to use words to build a person up. You will want them to not pass up a chance to bring joy and life into someone's day.

You will also work to drive out of their mouths their natural propensity to tear down or to build themselves up by tearing others down. You will want them to stop putting down strangers and interrupting when others are speaking.

You will work, seemingly with no progress, to teach them to hold back what they really want to say, to keep those words and thoughts in their head.

FROM MOM: Speak life.

WORDS CHECKLIST

- Do you have trouble saying the right thing at the right time?

- Do you often regret some of the things you say to others?

- Do you want to be a blessing to others by using your words?

- Progress will be slow, but the effort to help your kids use words wisely is worth it.

- Love for others should drive all of us to use our words to bless others.

did not of which
leaving you
did I do, have, you mus
my real feeling of this mo
commence
approache
offer. Caroline I am
from perceived not
I have nervous are
moment love
Caroline My dearest Ca
tear

VALUES

The Value of Purpose

The Value of Respect

The Value of Diligence

The Value of Self-Discipline

The Value of Humility

The Value of Being a Lifetime Learner

The Value of Generosity

The Value of Marriage

The Value of Faith

The Value of Righteousness

The Value of Words

The Value of Love

The Value of Thinking for Yourself

The Value of Traditions

The Value of Hospitality

The Value of Purity

Chapter 15

THE SECRET TO HAVING GOOD FRIENDS

"Positions are temporary. Ranks and titles are limited. But the way you treat people will always be remembered."

—Unknown

"I love you, you love me, we're a happy family."

—Barney

THE VALUE OF LOVE

Monday, November 12, 2012. Our family of six woke up with great expectations for this day, having hit our Orlando vacation in stride. We were on day five of a ten-day, once-in-a-lifetime Disney World experience. You kids were at the perfect ages: two boys at ten and twelve, two girls at six and eight.

We had visited each of the parks over the previous four days, with time off in between to relax, and today was the day we were going back to the Magic Kingdom. We were pumped! All of us had our own agenda to make this day the best of the entire trip. And, surprisingly, we were all on the same page.

The weather was a perfect 72 degrees and partly sunny. We were well rested. We knew our way around. By now, we were seasoned park-goers. We were going to suck every single second of life out of this day, and we were going to sleep tonight with huge smiles on our faces.

We rode the attractions and had lunch with princesses. There were *no lines*; we got to ride Space Mountain ten times! Our lunch was perfectly timed, with no wait, either. The stars had all lined up for our little family.

If there has ever been a *perfect* day at the *perfect* place, this was it. Disney could have used our family for a marketing campaign!

We had started the day early and left only after we watched the Main Street Electrical Parade, when the park was closing. Our vantage point for the parade was perfect. Our snacks had held us over between meals. Shoot, we didn't even get ice cream on any of our clothes! We had spent *all* day at the park and done everything we wanted to do, with no complaining, no lines, and no problems.

You can probably tell where this is going, right?

We had booked a two-room connected suite at one of Disney's spectacular resorts. On the shuttle ride back, everyone was smiling and laughing. Even the bus driver noticed just how happy we all were. Giggling, laughing, telling stories—our joy was contagious!

At the resort, we made the short walk to the main elevator to return to our third-story room. And that's when the rug of happiness was finally pulled out from under us.

"I call pushing the elevator button!" yelled eight-year-old Emma.

The utter delight of pushing elevator buttons is lost on most adults, but to kids, there is no greater honor than getting to light up that little button and direct the elevator where to go. No dessert, cartoon, or surprise birthday pony seems to compare to pushing that button. And when you "call" doing something, you get to do it. It's the law.

And then Levi broke that law when he jumped in front of her and pushed it first.

All. Hell. Broke. Loose.

In the middle of the main floor foyer.

Of a fully booked All-Star Disney resort.

At midnight.

That's right, our perfect day of joy, laughter, and family bonding came to a screeching halt over an elevator button.

Happiness is circumstantial. It can change in a heartbeat, like the half second it takes your older brother to steal the thing you "called." Happiness is easy to attain and even easier to lose.

I took Levi by the collar, dragged him down the hallway to our room, and closed and locked the door behind us. The rest of the family was left to sit quietly, heads down in a grade-school tornado warning position, while I had a very important meeting with my ten-year-old son.

After that incredible day when everything went our way, we were all so happy. But the instant something bad happened, we weren't happy anymore. As I scolded Levi for violating the "I call" rule, he was no longer happy. As Emma fumed in the hallway, she was no longer happy. As the rest of the family sat with an irate Emma, they weren't happy, either. Twelve hours of pure happiness were overwritten by one little finger pushing an elevator button.

That is the fragile nature of happiness: It can evaporate with one wrong move, even on the best day of your life.

Here's the key thing to note: Happiness and joy are *not* the same thing.

Happiness is fleeting. This story is a great example. We were all happy—until we weren't. Happiness is largely about what we take.

Joy, on the other hand, is about what we *give*. It comes from inner peace, and the world takes notice. Joy isn't circumstantial.

And for those of us who are followers of Christ, the Lord provides a quiet joy even in the midst of terrible life issues.

We know people who are going through chemotherapy; they have lost all their hair and are sick for three out of every four weeks. Their circumstances are terrible, but their attitude doesn't reflect that. They laugh, participate in lighthearted conversation, and sit at the dinner table with their family, even when they have no appetite. These people probably are not happy, but they are filled with an inner joy that is contagious.

We have a friend named April Langford. Her favorite color is yellow, like the sun, because sunshine brings joy. She smiles constantly. She and her husband, Ty, have two daughters, and both of them have the middle name Joy. April is full of joy all the time. That's not to say she doesn't occasionally feel sad or frustrated with her kids or lonely when Ty is deployed. But her circumstances never take away her overall joy.

> *"This is the day that the Lord has made; let us rejoice and be glad in it." (Psalm 118:24)*

The importance of "calling"—whether pushing an elevator button, riding shotgun, or grabbing the last slice of pizza—has since faded. We have all put the "Disney incident" behind us; you kids have grown up, and more important ideas have taken root in your hearts. We pray that as you kids mature, that selfish mentality will continue to be replaced by an others-first mentality, and your external happiness will be replaced by unshakable inner joy.

So what is the main difference between happiness and joy?

We believe the difference is *love*: love of others, putting others first, not loving yourself more than others, loving people when they are otherwise unlovely. The choice to love is what fills life with joy rather than just happiness.

Love centers your perspective on something bigger than your own emotions or fleeting desires. Joy can grow or shrink based on the quality of your relationships. Truly loving your siblings and your friends and having them love you back is one of the greatest joys in life.

We love you kids, and we know you love us. Yes, there are times when we don't all agree. That's to be expected. But through our whole family life—the diapers, the late nights, the teenage angst, the Disney meltdowns—our love for each other has kept growing in indescribable ways.

Think about that: With all the words available to us in our language (including the made-up words in the Urban Dictionary), it is pretty near impossible for something to be truly "indescribable."

Even so, I sometimes struggle to convey my deepest feelings for the people I love the most. None of the words I know come close.

We moved to Cookeville, Tennessee, in early 2009, and it didn't take us long to realize we had hit the jackpot of hiking trails and waterfalls.

We live seven miles, a ten-minute drive, from Burgess Falls State Park. This has been the first place we show visiting friends and family who want a taste of the great Tennessee outdoors. It has also been our go-to "we have nothing else to do" place to go hiking.

The Burgess Falls River Trail is only one and a half miles long round-trip, yet it has four fantastic waterfalls, each one bigger and more beautiful than the last.

We can go to Burgess Falls, hike the whole trail, and drive back home, all in less than one hour.

The whole park itself could be thought of as indescribable. But I have a more specific example in mind.

One winter day, you boys and I were hiking at Burgess Falls when we stumbled upon an area where water was dripping from the rivulets off the aptly named Falling Water River. It was below freezing that day, so icicles were forming in various shapes and sizes.

Then Levi saw it: a huge icicle, probably almost four feet long!

He was so excited about it that he insisted we take it home.

We reversed course and backtracked to the car, hauling the icicle between us. We kept the heater off on the drive home so it wouldn't melt. When we got home, we had to clear out space in the freezer to make room for the icicle. That was all a lot of work for a pointy piece of frozen water!

What was the big deal?

Why did Levi want to bring that icicle home so badly?

Because he wanted his mom to see it, too. And that alone was obviously worth the effort.

We know you kids love us, and crazy gestures like saving an icicle for us are how you show it.

This is what's so indescribable about the love shared between a parent and child: We can't explain how it makes us feel when a small child goes *way* out of their way to show you something just so they can see the joy on your face.

That said, for every grand gesture like bringing an icicle home, there are probably thousands of little gestures and actions that go unacknowledged all the time.

I'm sure everyone alive on earth right now desires some type of affirmation. It doesn't always have to be a big deal; sometimes it's just nice to know that somebody noticed your effort. And we can give that to the people in our own circles.

Instead of saying "You didn't do it right," or "Isn't that what you get paid for?" you can choose to say, "You did a great job," and "Thank you!" It may not seem like much, but it can make someone's entire day.

A parent's job is to encourage their kids to be the best version of themselves. When you see them take a step in that direction because of the love they have received *from* you, the love they feel *for* you, and their realization that other people in this world matter, well, that feeling is … **indescribable!**

I hate to admit this, but I almost hated your Uncle Jack when we were growing up together. We "called" everything, and while I was bigger, stronger, and faster, he was smarter. He figured things out before me and often got the better of me. My overinflated pride was hurt numerous times when he would prank me, outwit me, or outflank me. For several years, we had an adversarial relationship. But over the last couple of decades, I have grown to love him (and his family, of course) so much that just writing these words brings me joy.

Your mom and I also have friends who bring us joy. It is hard work keeping a friendship going when roads diverge, but the joy those friendships bring us is worth the effort.

We encourage you to put in the work to be friends with your siblings and to foster other meaningful friendships outside your family. As Proverbs 18:24 says, "A man of many companions may come to ruin, but there is a friend that sticks closer than a brother."

You can choose your friends, but you can't choose your family.

Prioritize your family. Love your future sisters- and brothers-in-law. Care for your future nieces and nephews. Reach out to your cousins. Family may not always feel easy, but it's the foundation that teaches us how to show up for others.

As far as friends go, you all have good ones now, but that hasn't always been true. We used to walk you through how to choose your friends.

In this world, we encounter so many different types of people.

Some are quiet.

Some are loud.

Some are easily excitable.

Some are chill all the time.

When it comes to deciding which people to *intentionally* spend time with, we have always sorted people into three categories.

GREEN

People that we categorize as "green" are the people who almost *always* brighten your day and make you smile. They have energy that lifts you up. These people can come in all sorts of personalities, but what they have in common is that you usually feel better after spending time with them. There is literally *no limit* to the time you can spend with (or, I should say, invest in) these people.

YELLOW

People that we have frequently classified as "yellow" *can* be positive, but they can also be negative. These people seem to have a quality that's difficult to pinpoint; you only know that at the end of the day, you feel like you should limit your time with them. In other words, they require caution. I would say these are easily the most difficult people to identify and make the necessary adjustments to be around. There may not be that many issues with them, but there is always an undercurrent of negativity. These are the people who might bring drama, sarcasm, passive aggression, or distraction to your relationship, but only occasionally. Your gut will often know them before your mind does.

RED

Toxic. Poison. Venom. The people who fall into the "red" category need to be eliminated from your life. If they are related to you, then you need to limit any and all time you spend with them. These folks are not good, and you know it. If I asked you to identify someone like this and a name or face popped into your mind immediately, you should take that as a red flag.

As you get to know people in your workplace, you will be able to sort your coworkers into these categories. It is wise to control your workflow and breaks to limit your time around the people labelled "red" and "yellow" and increase your time with the "green" people.

We sit down with you kids at the end of every year and ask each of you to identify who in your life is "green." Then we ask you to make it a priority to find ways to spend more time with those people.

If anyone in your life has slid from "green" to "yellow," we encourage you to cut back on your time with them.

Finally, we ask you to identify who the "red" people are in your lives. Every time we have asked this question, you've had an answer. Oftentimes, you just needed some type of permission to pull away from what you already knew deep down was a toxic relationship.

FROM MOM: I love you all so much, I want to squeeze you right now as I write this. You bring me more joy than anything or anyone else. I want you to come back to visit us. My "love tank" will be refilled every time you come back. But I will also encourage all of you to invest in deep, "green" friendships. I am blessed with so many friends who love me and whom I love; they multiply my joy. My greatest source of joy is my relationship with Jesus. When I was around ten years old, my family and I attended a revival, and it was then that I first realized my need for Jesus. During the response time after the service was complete, I felt my heart pounding; I knew I needed to make a decision to follow Christ. As the song played, I stepped out of the pew into the aisle and floated the rest of the way up. That day was a step in the right direction. A little later, maybe a week or two, your Mamaw and I were at a friend's house. Her name was Jean Thigpen, and she was one of my mom's mentors. On the way home, I asked questions about Jesus, salvation, and going to Heaven. After we got home, I sat on our rusty brown couch and Mamaw prayed with me while I asked Jesus to come into my heart. That source of joy has been in my heart ever since. It brings us joy, too, that all of you have made that same choice.

LOVE CHECKLIST

- Where are your kids on the red/yellow/green scale? Where are you?

- Do you or your kids know of a "red" friend who is making a negative impact?

- Are you joyful or just "happy"?

- Following Christ is the only way, in our opinion, to be filled with joy all the time.

- You will never regret loving people and showing them love.

VALUES

The Value of Purpose

The Value of Respect

The Value of Diligence

The Value of Self-Discipline

The Value of Humility

The Value of Being a Lifetime Learner

The Value of Generosity

The Value of Marriage

The Value of Faith

The Value of Righteousness

The Value of Words

The Value of Love

The Value of Thinking for Yourself

The Value of Traditions

The Value of Hospitality

The Value of Purity

Chapter 16

AREN'T ALL HOMESKOOLED KIDS WEIRD?

"Little minds are tamed and subdued by misfortunes; but great minds rise above them."

—WASHINGTON IRVING

THE VALUE OF THINKING FOR YOURSELF

Admittedly, when you were kids, homeschooling was uncommon. We only knew a few families who were homeschooling, and all of them were one step away from living an Amish lifestyle. All, that is, except for one: the Wades. The couple who had the greatest influence on us when we were impressionable first-time parents were James and Betsy Wade. They homeschooled their kids, and they were normal (well, at least compared to stereotypical homeschool families).

We love the Wade family to this day and appreciate the way they modeled good homeschooling. As you kids know, your Mamaw, Papaw, Grandad, aunt, uncle, and cousins on your mom's side are or were public school teachers. There is a great misunderstanding about homeschooling from the public-school sector. They almost feel insulted. And I get it. They must assume homeschool parents think they can teach their kids better—even though public schools have more resources and an environment specifically designed for education.

We admit we were skeptical. Certainly, a man with a degree in business and a woman with a degree in exercise science couldn't do a better job of educating their kids than trained teachers, right?

We have some dear friends who are public school teachers. I would love to name them here, but we know so many that we would certainly leave someone out by accident. We wish they could have taught you all. Yet in the end, we chose to homeschool you, and we wanted to explain why.

Our decision to homeschool was 100 percent driven by our desire to be the primary influencers in your life. We felt so strongly about instilling our values in you, the same values we've written about in this book.

There was no other reason. No ulterior motive.

We did not, for example, think that we could do a better job than all of our public-school friends. We did not choose to homeschool because we wanted to give you a purely Christian education or focus on Greek or Latin or the Classical

Conversations curriculum that is prominent in homeschooling today. While all those things are great, that is *not* **why we made** our **decision.**

It also wasn't about fear of violence, like school shootings and other horrific events frequently in the news. While we did want to keep you safe, we knew (as we mentioned in Chapter 12) that we couldn't protect you all the time. Your lives are in God's hands.

Instead, our decision was based on love. We had been praying about raising godly kids who would make a difference in this world. We have said many times that we wanted to raise kids who would be part of the world's solutions, not the world's problems. We continued to debate this idea until Max was old enough for kindergarten.

At that time, I (Dad) was still working in finance. I would drive to the bank and back listening to a radio station broadcasting from Black Mountain, North Carolina. It was a Christian radio station that would often play sermons by Chip Ingram, David Jeremiah, and Greg Laurie. During my commute, the daily talk show by *Focus on the Family* would be on the air. (*Focus on the Family* is a ministry that was founded by James Dobson, and at the time, he hosted the radio program.) I listened to sermons and to this program every day I drove to work, and these men, who I will never meet, had a great influence on my spiritual thought process.

One day, I was wrestling with the idea that I needed to leave banking and go into church work to be a pastor. I struggled mightily through that process, so much so that it took me a few years to make that decision.

At the time, we were attending First Baptist Church in Morristown, Tennessee. I was the chairman of the personnel committee, and our pastor, Randy Davis, had asked us to put together a job description for a new pastoral position at FBC. We worked on this as a committee for weeks, maybe months. At some point, I felt a strong sense that God was calling me to apply for that very position.

As I drove back and forth to work, listening to the radio, I began fretting over the decision to throw my hat in the ring. I was sure the job didn't pay as much as the bank did, and I knew, having grown up in the home of a pastor, that my life would change.

There was also the fact that when your mom and I had been dating for over a year and were started to get serious, she made one thing very clear: "Lee, I have not been called to be a pastor's wife."

"Well, that's fine," I said, "because I have not been called to be a pastor."

We had never spoken of it again since then, but as I worked on this project with the personnel committee, that conversation resurfaced in my mind. I worried that Mom wouldn't like this "calling" I was giving ear to, that she was afraid to be a pastor's wife. So I kept my idea from her for a long time.

In retrospect, that was silly. Truth be told, she was feeling a pull at the same time I was. Not that she felt "worthy" of being a pastor's wife—whatever that means—but that she felt like God was leading me away from banking. When I finally discussed the job opportunity with her, she was responsive, sweet, and nothing but encouraging.

What does this have to do with homeschooling, you might ask? Well, after I told Mom about my feelings, a great burden was lifted from my shoulders. One day, as I was riding high on my commute, a conversation came up on the *Focus on the Family* show about dads being more involved in raising their kids. As I listened, I realized that our desire to be the primary influencers in the lives of our kids would dovetail really well with a more family-friendly and less commute-heavy job.

In that moment, I began to cry softly. I believed that God was telling us to homeschool our kids by offering me a way to be a better help to Mom, who would obviously be the head teacher in our newly formed Bailey Academy.

This would be our opportunity to do what we said we wanted to do: instill good values in our kids. Homeschooling wasn't about rejecting traditional schools; it was about embracing responsibility.

Homeschooling is hard—especially with four school-age kids under eleven. But we were up for the challenge.

NO-MEDIA MONDAYS

It didn't take us long to figure out that any and all things in the house that *can* distract, *will*. So we instituted what we called "no-media Mondays." This was a strict rule: no music, no TV, no video games, no phones, no noise of any kind. Not even church music was allowed, only the sounds of work and your own voices. We wanted silence to make room for focus and imagination and to help reset the pace of the week.

What happened on Mondays? Creativity! You boys spent multiple Mondays crafting with paper, wood, plastic, and any other material you could find to make a full homemade chess set, which you then played games of chess with. We loved it!

You kids played outside on Mondays more than any other day of the week. More games were created and played on Mondays, too. Bicycles were ridden more often and more treats were baked. Mondays gave you the most freedom from electronic devices.

NO-TV TUESDAY

Tuesdays were like Mondays, except that we did allow music. This opened up room for dance and karaoke parties. Rapping, singing, and dancing were common on Tuesdays, along with the creative activities you also did on Mondays.

Of course, you had school, too. That was usually right after breakfast. The fundamentals of school—reading, writing, math, and history—were all subjects that were not only taught but incorporated into daily life.

SCHEDULE?

Some people have asked us about our homeschool schedule. The truth is that we didn't really have one, but this is how our days usually went:

Monday through Friday, I (Mom) taught classes at the local YMCA. The Y had childcare that started at 8 a.m. Dad usually went to the gym early, around 6 a.m. I would get up around 7 a.m. and make a small breakfast for myself. Once you kids were old enough, I let you wake up on your own—unless you slept in, otherwise we would be late. Sometimes you would make your own breakfast, but we also had cereal bars for you to grab on the way out. Once we got to the YMCA, you would play there from 8 to 10 a.m. while I taught my classes.

On Mondays, Tuesdays, and Wednesdays, we would then come back home for your lessons. (This was when those of you who didn't eat a good breakfast would run to the kitchen for a snack.)

Once everyone was fed and settled, we started school around 10:45 a.m. Each of you worked independently; it wasn't like a one-room schoolhouse with me standing up front and pointing at an old chalkboard. You all had lists to memorize from, like state capitals and books of the Bible, which we had you work on for several minutes every day.

You also had workbooks for each subject: math, science, English, and social studies. We almost always had something for you to read. Since you worked independently, you were rarely all in the same room. I would walk around the house and make sure you were all working on your studies. You had the freedom to choose which subject to work on first; part of our goal was to teach you how to figure things out on your own. The workbooks came with instructions, but if you still needed help, you could always come to us.

The middle of the day was when we taught you "home economics." This wasn't random; after an hour of poring over your workbooks, you were always good and hungry for lunch, so it was the perfect time to teach you skills like cooking and cleaning.

Just as with breakfast, each of you was responsible for making your own lunch. It was up to you what you ate, whether a peanut butter and jelly sandwich or a five-course meal. This made the kitchen a disaster area, of course, but we wanted you to learn things by *doing* them.

Chores often came after lunchtime, so schoolwork often resumed around 2 p.m. You were expected to focus on your workbooks from 2 to 4 p.m. (although, to be honest, that wasn't always the case).

Thursdays were different: After I finished teaching my classes at the YMCA, we did our family grocery shopping together. This was a great opportunity to teach you kids about food costs, allow you to (safely) be independent, and let you practice responsibility; you looked forward to helping me build the shopping list, find the items on our coupons, and compare prices to make sure we were saving money. To this day, you remember Thursdays most fondly.

On Fridays, Dad was home, so you could sleep in if you wanted. I had his help if I needed it, and we would try to wrap up by noon.

Looking at this "schedule" now, you might think we didn't do very much "formal" schooling. I guess that's true. We did know going in that homeschooling would be different from public school education. Only time will tell if it was the right choice.

FROM DAD: Kids, we do acknowledge that teaching you to be independent thinkers came with pros and cons. You can figure things out for yourself, but you also often think our words of wisdom are outdated ("People don't do things like that anymore, Dad."). We have butted heads time and again, and I admit I sometimes wish you would just accept my advice without question. That would certainly be easier.

Your independence makes some things more complicated. You have ideas, dreams, thoughts, and feelings that your mom and I may not agree with. Sometimes you make decisions out of (over)confidence without thinking about the long-term consequences.

Sometimes your minds scare us a little. More than anything, though, they excite us.

FROM MOM: If I'm honest, homeschooling is the area of parenting where I feel the most insecure. We worked on life skills but didn't spend as much time as your public-school peers studying World War II or the nervous system or the periodic table. None of you did as well on the ACT as your friends did. We had to have faith that it would all even out in the end—because if it didn't, it would be my fault. (Your dad doesn't let me talk like that, but that is how I feel sometimes.)

THINKING FOR YOURSELF CHECKLIST

- Are you willing to give up something important in order to live out one of your values?

- Are you afraid to homeschool your kids because you feel inadequate?

- Are you willing to structure your days around your values?

- Homeschooling is hard, but we believe it was worth the investment.

- Think for yourself.

VALUES

The Value of Purpose

The Value of Respect

The Value of Diligence

The Value of Self-Discipline

The Value of Humility

The Value of Being a Lifetime Learner

The Value of Generosity

The Value of Marriage

The Value of Faith

The Value of Righteousness

The Value of Words

The Value of Love

The Value of Thinking for Yourself

The Value of Traditions

The Value of Hospitality

The Value of Purity

Chapter 17

NO SANTA, NO EASTER BUNNY, NO TOOTH FAIRY

"Family isn't a noun. It's a verb requiring action
from each member to keep the whole afloat."

—UNKNOWN

THE VALUE OF FAMILY TRADITIONS

It was one of our first Christmases as a couple, and we were invited to join another family for their Christmas gathering. There was one small child in the family who was opening gifts, and as it happens, the first three of them were clothes instead of toys. The little boy's father, in an attempt to quiet a disgruntled child who had been hyped up about the loot, said to one of his family members, "Find this kid a toy *now*!" We can still remember how jarring that moment felt. A child who had been taught to expect magic and mountains of gifts was suddenly disappointed and being treated like a problem to be fixed. It wasn't about the child, really. It was about what the moment revealed: a holiday built more on pressure and expectations than on meaning or relationships.

Your mom and I found that so distasteful that we decided to create a more purposeful Christmas tradition for our own future family.

You kids will have your own experiences that influence how you do birthdays, Christmas, Easter, and other holidays and traditions. We admit we struggled to find our footing for the first few years; we just did what everyone told us to do. Sometimes that meant we overdid it. Other times we held back. We hadn't yet filtered our actions through the lens of our values, and that's what made the difference later.

Eventually, we came up with traditions of our own, as you all know so well. In this chapter, we wanted to walk you through each of our traditions and why we established them the way we did. At the same time, we want you to know that while we had our own reasoning, we aren't going to disown you if you don't follow in our footsteps. You need to create your own traditions. Don't just do something because we or your spouse's family did things that way. Do it because it reinforces a value that is important to you. One day, you'll have the chance to explain to your kids what your family traditions meant.

BIRTHDAYS

We very well may have dropped the ball on these events. Our philosophy was pretty harsh. We didn't do a good job of making birthdays *"big"* like some families do. Looking back, it would have been a good excuse to get the family together. Instead, we felt birthdays were days when you should be recognized, but not celebrated.

Personally, I think that I (Dad) had too much influence on this one, while your mom would have preferred to throw a few more parties. I wanted to celebrate accomplishments, character milestones, and life events like your first job or your wedding. I would rather get excited about you being asked to lead in prayer at a banquet or going out of your way to help a friend in need than you surviving another trip around the sun. I wanted to celebrate who you were becoming rather than the number of years you'd been on Earth. Looking back, though, I understand that the years themselves were worth honoring, too, simply because they were yours.

FROM MOM: This is one area in which I completely disagreed with your dad. I believed in giving you special attention on your birthday. We made your favorite dinner, we had cake or ice cream, and we always gave you presents. We also threw *big* parties for your fifth and tenth birthdays, as well as your **Golden Birthdays.**

(For those who don't know what a Golden Birthday is, it's the birthday that corresponds with the day of the month you were born: Max's eleventh birthday on August 11; Levi's and

Audrey's fourteenth on January 14 and August 14, respectively; and Emma's tenth on February 10.)

What did a Golden Birthday celebration consist of? Theme parks, water parks, ice skating, much bigger presents (like a TV). We made the Golden Birthday an experience!

HIGH SCHOOL GRADUATION

I (Dad) was even more harsh about the whole high school graduation thing. When I graduated from high school, I sent out dozens and dozens of invitations. If I'm being honest, I didn't expect anyone besides my own parents and maybe grandparents to attend my ceremony. The invitations, therefore, felt more like requests for college starter money.

I was incredibly appreciative of the responses, but I still look back on that time with mixed emotions. I didn't really work hard in high school. In fact, I goofed off. Yet I was in the top ten percent academically. All I had to do was make it to school on time and complete most of my assignments. Why would anyone give me money for that?

This idea carried over into our parenting. I would disagree with your mom about invitations and announcements: "Why should we celebrate the bare minimum achievement of making it through the American education system?"

That sounds harsh, but I know how easy it was for you all to finish high school. I'd rather celebrate you overcoming challenges at work and being promoted, achievements that are actually difficult.

Your mom doesn't agree with me, of course. When you get married and have in-laws with different family traditions, know that after reflection, I might agree. We will probably do things differently with your kids.

But don't even get me started on Valentine's Day....

SPRING BREAK

As a homeschool family, we had 100 percent flexibility when it came to vacations. That's why we never went anywhere during the crowded spring break and fall break weeks or Fourth of July weekend. We didn't want to camp or travel at the same time everyone else was. We know you missed out on some beach and ski trips because of this, but maybe someday you'll understand how important avoiding crowds is in the Bailey family.

MOTHER'S DAY/FATHER'S DAY

We never wanted to guilt or pressure you into celebrating us. We feel it is our responsibility to celebrate our anniversary and to make each other feel special on Mother's Day and Father's Day. That said, whenever you reach out to your mom or visit her on her birthday or Mother's Day, you should know she lights up like a lighthouse on a moonless night.

In other words, we never want a relationship built on obligation. But a simple thoughtful gesture—a card, a call, a kind word—means more than you can imagine. Even small gestures are sacred when made from the heart.

CHRISTMAS

We came under more scrutiny for this stance than for any other tradition we've created. We chose to never mention Santa Claus, *ever*. We didn't villainize him, but we didn't celebrate him, either. Why? Why were we so willing to swim against a very strong current? Well, where else would you kids learn about the true meaning of Christmas if not at home? This wasn't about being contrarian or trying to ruin anyone's holiday. It was about focus. We knew that if we didn't take an active role in shaping the story you kids absorbed about Christmas, then the cultural noise would drown out the deeper message.

The way we see it, an individual's worldview is shaped by three independent sources: the outside world, their social circle (church, friends, school, etc.), and their homelife.

We knew that the world at large would almost exclusively give you the Santa story, with very little focus on the Nativity story about the birth of Jesus. So there went one-third of your worldview.

As for your social circles, we also felt we couldn't count on them to teach you about the spiritual meaning of Christmas—not even church. Sunday school teachers would give a stale, cookie-cutter lesson about Jesus' birth, only to ask you what Santa was bringing you for Christmas the moment class was over. In fact, that was the most commonly asked question to our kids at church, at the gym play area, and at family and friends' homes. That disconnect was hard to reconcile. How could we reinforce the deeper meaning of Jesus' arrival while everyone, even well-meaning adults, drew your attention away toward an imaginary man in a red suit?

After much consideration, we came to this sobering conclusion: If we did not spend 100 percent of our efforts educating you on the birth of Jesus, then every Christmas, you would only ever care about Santa Claus. That would be a parenting fail in our book.

EASTER BUNNY/TOOTH FAIRY

Friends who heard about our approach to Santa Claus would sometimes try to catch us off guard: "Okay, if you aren't going to lie to your kids, then what are you going to tell them about the Easter Bunny or the Tooth Fairy?"

The former was easy: If we could avoid mentioning Santa to teach you kids about Jesus' birth, we could certainly avoid mentioning the much less popular Easter Bunny to teach you about His resurrection. We did, of course, let you eat chocolate eggs on Easter (we're not monsters!), but we chose to forgo the Easter egg hunts so we could focus on the biblical story of Easter that means so much to our faith.

The Tooth Fairy is a different matter. We probably would have just gone along with the traditional story had our friends not challenged us about "lying" to our kids. If we were going to be honest about Santa, wouldn't we need to do the same with the Tooth Fairy?

So we put our heads together and came up with an alternative that was honest and, frankly, *tons* **more fun**: the tooth prize tradition! We told you that whenever you lost a tooth, we would come into your room in the middle of the night to take it from under your pillow. If we were able to take the tooth without waking you up, we would leave a small prize. If, however, you were able to catch us in the act, we would leave you a much larger and more expensive prize. This turned an otherwise passive tradition into an interactive game that made you feel involved, empowered, and excited, even when you knew the truth.

From Max's first lost tooth through many of Audrey's, the game. Was. *On*! The dozens of ways that you all tried to stay awake or booby-trap the room so we'd make too much noise was both hilarious and impressive. You rigged alarms, set traps, and staged decoys. What started as a way to avoid a lie became one of our most treasured traditions.

In Chapter 15, we talked about loving each other. It was during one of our "Tooth Fairy" escapades that we witnessed Levi and Emma's love for one another, even though that love is often overshadowed by competition.

By the time Emma got her turn in the Tooth Fairy game, she had witnessed many of her older brothers' attempts to catch us and get the bigger tooth prize. She saw Levi up the ante numerous times, to the point where Mom and I had to spend thirty minutes or more avoiding booby traps and other obstacles.

Emma thought she was ready. She talked a big game, but we both knew she was the heaviest sleeper in the house, not to mention she went to bed earlier than anyone else. Mom and I had zero concerns about waking her up. We knew we could sneak into her room half an hour after she went to bed, make the exchange, and sneak back out, and she would be none the wiser. This wasn't our first rodeo, either; we had the timing and stealth down to a science. We thought this would be the easiest game yet.

At first, everything went according to plan. Then, just as we were sneaking into Emma's bedroom, a loud *thud* startled us! In a panic, we retreated into the hallway and closed the door. Where was that noise coming from? After a minute, it stopped. We went back in, but the noise started again, louder and faster.

That's when we figured it out: Levi and Max's room was next to Emma and Audrey's room, and their bunk beds shared a wall. Levi was banging on the wall—the same wall Emma was sleeping next to—to wake her up! He was working "undercover" for his sister! Levi nearly punched through that wall trying to wake Emma—and it was all Mom and I could do not to laugh and accidentally help his efforts.

In the end, Emma slept through the night and got the small prize for her tooth. But since that day, we knew, even if it wasn't always obvious, that those two cared for each other. This tooth prize memory is one of our favorites.

In truth, we could probably write an entire book of stories from the "Tooth Fairy" game alone. You may have outgrown the game, but we never outgrew the joy of watching your creative minds at work. That tradition taught us that the best memories are born from laughter, teamwork, and a little mischief.

LONG DAY, THE GRANDEST OF ALL TRADITIONS

This is the tradition that truly defines our family.

A small notebook still in my office. My first real job. The weird way I (Dad) organize my life.

My first real "big-boy" job was at a bank. Eventually, I would accumulate fifteen years of experience in banking, but at first, it was just a way to make ends meet.

What I noticed about all the suit-wearing, high-powered executives was that they usually didn't work late or on weekends.

I discovered something interesting about the banking industry: Business can't be done unless a bank is open. You need tellers, you need processors, you need the vault to be unlocked. The bank observed all the government holidays (they're called "bank holidays" for a reason), so if there was a big, important deal you were ready to close on Columbus Day, you just had to wait.

This is where I got the idea to create a holiday exclusively for our family. All the bigwigs at the bank would stop whatever they were working on when even a minor holiday came around.

So, we decided to do the same thing.

We would aside a day of the year and observe that "holiday" *no matter what*.

When I first started my job at the bank, I wanted to be thoughtful and organized. Every time a major thought crossed my mind, one that I knew would be important later in life, I would figure out a way to capture that thought. After much trial and error, I finally had a notebook, complete with a table of contents.

It was 1995, two years after Mom and I got married, and it occurred to me that June had the longest day of the year: the summer solstice. I jotted that thought down as a note in my little notebook.

It sat there for two years before we finally decided to do something to mark the longest day of the year.

Maybe it was because in 1997, that day fell on a Saturday. Maybe it just took that long to get serious about the idea. Maybe we had nothing else to do, so we decided to go for a hike on what happened to be the longest day of the year. We didn't start with a grand plan. We simply took one idea and acted on it. That's often how the most meaningful traditions are born.

Whatever the reason, "Long Day" was created.

That day in 1997, we went on a long hike, had a picnic, and enjoyed the sunrise and sunset. We took our dog, Jazmine, with us. I remember a photo we took together that day at Elrod Falls in Sneedville, Tennessee. It was the only photo of our first Long Day, but after years of looking for it, Mom and I still haven't found it.

We know we also celebrated Long Day in 1998 and 1999, but we can't find any photos or notes from then, either. We do know we started something special, though!

So what exactly is Long Day?

While it started off in 1997 with a nice hike, we didn't know yet how it was all going to play out.

But we started. That is how you make family traditions: Start them. Start lots of them. Be creative and flexible. Some will stick, and some will fade. Not every idea becomes a legacy. But you'll never know unless you try. Start small. Try something silly. If it works, great. If it flops, you've got a funny story.

Long Day, as we now celebrate it, is a day we attempt to fill with as many fun family activities as possible, from sunup to sundown, barely stopping to eat or drink. We *go, go, go* until someone cries or falls asleep.

Ice cream is a requirement. You don't have to want it, but you do have to eat it. (Seriously, though, who doesn't want ice cream?)

We have often said that Long Day isn't complete until we've had ice cream, someone has cried at least once, and someone has said, ironically or not, "Whew, it's been a looooong day!"

Some Long Days are more epic than others, but as a whole, this unique family holiday holds some of our fondest memories.

Here's an example of a typical Long Day:

LONG DAY ITINERARY 2007

4:00 a.m. – Wake everyone up

4:30 a.m. – Still try to wake everyone up

5:00 a.m. – Everyone is out of bed, watch the sun rise

5:45 a.m. – Leave home in Alabama, drive to Nashville Zoo

7:00 a.m. – Stop for breakfast at IHOP

8:45 a.m. – Arrive at Nashville Zoo, be first in line

9:00 a.m. – Enter zoo, breeze through, leave

10:00 a.m. – Back in van, drive to Louisville, Kentucky (eat premade snacks in car en route)

2:00 p.m. – [Time zone change] Arrive at Louisville Zoo

2:05 p.m. – Bathroom breaks, run through zoo and try to see something we didn't see in Nashville

3:30 p.m. – Leave zoo, head to Louisville Slugger Museum

5:05 p.m. – Arrive five minutes after closing to Schimpff's Confectionery in Jeffersonville, Indiana, one of the oldest candy stores in the country. (We returned to see it in 2025.)

5:15 p.m. – Leave Louisville, drive to Cincinnati, Ohio

7:00 p.m. – Run through Creation Museum before closing

8:30 p.m. – Check in to hotel

9:30 p.m. – Go to local place in Cincinnati for ice cream

11:00 p.m. – Bedtime

9:00 a.m. – [Next day] Check out of hotel

10:00 a.m. – Go to Cincinnati Zoo

12:30 p.m. – Eat lunch at zoo

2:00 p.m. – Drive back home

This Long Day had us passing through five states, visiting three zoos and two museums, and doing all sorts of fun activities, all in a thirty-hour period. It was exhausting. It was chaotic. It was a logistical circus. But it was also unforgettable. There's something about shared fatigue, shared meals, shared detours, and shared laughter that bonds a family in ways regular days don't. You don't need a five-state trip to create this kind of memory; you just need a little effort, a little planning, and a lot of flexibility.

A CHARLIE BROWN THANKSGIVING

Regardless of what your own family did, there is some merit to considering *starting* something new!

I *love* Thanksgiving. I remember it fondly as the one day each year that I was guaranteed the chance to watch my favorite sports team on television. Growing up in the last house on a gravelly dead-end road in rural Tennessee, well before ESPN and NFL RedZone, we were completely at the mercy of the local TV stations, which got to air whatever games of whatever teams they wanted. Rarely did they choose the Dallas Cowboys.

But I knew I'd get to watch the Cowboys on Thanksgiving because they were the only team that played every year. (Okay, the Detroit Lions played too, but nobody in our house cared. Sorry, Lions fans.)

The shuffling around of people and plates never seemed to interfere with game time. For me, this was the greatest of all holidays: all family, food, and football, with none of the pressure of gift-giving.

It would have been easy to convince your mom never to touch Thanksgiving, to say the holiday is so full of traditions that it would be foolhardy to try anything new. After all, if it ain't broke...

Even so, about fifteen years into our marriage, when you kids were ages three to nine, we changed things up. We decided to try a Charlie Brown Thanksgiving.

In this thirty-minute TV special from the '70s, Charlie Brown is coerced into making Thanksgiving dinner for his friends. As usual for Peanuts, there are apparently no grown-ups anywhere in the zip code, so his dog Snoopy throws together an unconventional menu:

- Buttered toast
- Pretzels
- Jelly beans
- Popcorn
- Ice cream sundaes

(Good thing none of these unsupervised children used the oven, right?)

Every year since 2006, we have settled down in front of the television the day before Thanksgiving to watch this special and eat all the same food Snoopy makes. It's quirky. It's not nutritious. And it's absolutely perfect. The simplicity of the meal is what makes the tradition so fun. It's completely out of the ordinary!

We love this tradition and have even added to it over the years. For about ten years, we wore matching pajamas while enjoying our "nutritious" meal. When the boys mentioned they never wear pajamas, we pivoted to matching sweatshirts. We now invite our adopted family, the Allens, over and get to experience the jelly-beans-and-whipped-cream-in-the-face joy all over again.

MEMORIAL DAY

Who doesn't love holidays and time off work, right?

But if we're not taught what a day means, we can easily take it for granted. That used to be the case for Memorial Day.

Bankers look forward to government holidays because they're automatically paid days off. I never had to worry about working on New Year's Day, Martin Luther King Jr. Day, President's Day, Columbus Day, or any other bank holiday.

So to me, Memorial Day was just another day off.

I had no military background, no close family in service. I didn't attend parades or ceremonies growing up. All I knew about Memorial Day was that it was the start of summer and a good excuse to grill burgers.

When I was around ten years old, my father was a bivocational pastor of a small Baptist church in a dairy farming community in east Tennessee. We knew everyone in town. One day, a new kid arrived on the scene. He was about twelve or thirteen, and as I recall, he was chubby and smoked cigarettes.

Due to some odd family dynamics, he had moved to our little town to live with his grandmother and be near his aunt and uncle. I remember him being a rough kid, *clearly* not from our neck of the woods.

His aunt and uncle attended our little church, so he was practically forced to attend. In a short period of time—I believe tanks to family and the wonderful influence of the adults in our church community—he found Jesus. For the first time in his life, he'd found purpose. He felt *alive*.

I had never witnessed such a radical outward change in someone so young. I watched as he transformed from a chubby kid who was rough around the edges to a chiseled athlete.

When I say he changed his life, I mean he *really* changed it. He swam in his aunt and uncle's above-ground pool and changed his diet so radically that everyone took notice. He began studying the Bible with fervor. He read books on Bible study, on getting into shape, on outdoorsmanship, and on swimming. He became dedicated, disciplined, and dependable. He was the first among us to get a job as a high school student. He would lead us on hikes and tell us about what he was learning in all of his studies—spiritual, physical, mental, nutritional, and occupational. He had a hunger to grow in body, mind, and soul. We all saw it. And it inspired the rest of us to step up, too.

He became a leader in his high school swim team and the de facto leader of our little youth group. At age sixteen, he was already a man among boys.

Meanwhile, I was the youngest member of the youth group and, by my own admission, the most impressionable. And that led me straight toward this kid: my new friend, Bill Bennett.

I went everywhere Bill would take me. We went hiking, caving, riding, biking, and swimming. I learned about tents, flashlights, and camo pants. I learned about bodyweight strength training and the joy that comes from personal discipline.

I spent the night at his place as often as I could. Several times, I helped him at his job as a tour guide for one of the largest underground caverns in the Great Smoky Mountains. I was introduced to the idea of being "carefully dangerous": We went caving and hiking in some extremely dangerous places, but Bill made us go slowly to mitigate the risk.

I also learned about leaving no trace. We took snacks on our day-long adventures, and Bill always brought an apple. During our break, he ate that apple whole, core and all.

I was only a rising junior in high school when Bill enlisted in the Army. And just like that, he was gone: off to boot camp, then deployed.

I am *so* glad I stuck by his side during the brief time I had with him.

Over the course of a nearly twenty-year career in the military, Bill became a leader among leaders everywhere he went. He was respected, trusted, needed, appreciated, decorated. These are the many honors he received:

- Silver Star Medal
- Bronze Star Medal with Valor Device
- Purple Heart
- Army Commendation Medal
- Army Achievement Medal

- Army Good Conduct Medal with Five Bronze Knots
- National Defense Service Medal
- Southwest Asia Service Medal
- Afghanistan Campaign Medal with Bronze Star
- Iraq Campaign Medal with Bronze Star
- Global War on Terrorism Expeditionary Medal
- Global War on Terrorism Service Medal
- Humanitarian Service Medal
- Army NCO Professional Development Ribbon
- Army Service Ribbon
- Army Overseas Service Ribbon
- Kuwait Liberation Medal (Saudi Arabia)
- Kuwait Liberation Medal (Kuwait)
- Combat Infantryman Badge with Star (Second Award)
- Parachutist Badge
- Special Operations Diver Badge
- Special Forces Tab

On rare occasions, Bill would come back home, and his uncle and aunt would invite all the boys from high school to visit him and his wife, Allison. All of us were at his wedding, and we were all pallbearers at his grandmother's funeral.

We stayed in touch as much as possible, but as the years passed, we saw him less and less.

SEPTEMBER 12, 2003

The terrorist attacks in New York and Pennsylvania on September 11, 2001, will forever be ingrained in the minds of every American alive to witness those awful events live on the news. It was because of those attacks that the US military beefed up its presence and aggression in the Middle East. By that time, Bill was a trained medic, a Green Beret Special Forces warrior, and the recipient of several miltary awards.

Two years later, almost to the day,, Bill was slated to have some time off, and our old group planned a small reunion. But things went sideways during his last raid before his leave, and his unit was ambushed.

Bill saw several of his men get picked off before he spotted the sniper. He gave his fallen men as much medical attention as possible, and once they were all out of danger, he climbed the tallest building in that area to go after the sniper. They shot each other at the same time, and both Bill and the sniper died.

In the wake of that loss, Memorial Day has taken on a new meaning for me.

Now it makes me think of Bill's widow, Allison, and the high regard and respect I have for her as she lives a life that would make him proud.

It makes me think of all the spouses and parents and children with loved ones in active service.

It makes me think of the men and women who have made sacrifices like Bill's, people I never met and whose names I will never know.

It makes me want to live up to my own potential because it's one of the freedoms that Bill died to protect.

I don't know how to honor someone like Bill. I don't even know how to thank his wife.

As a small token of my appreciation, each year on Memorial Day, I go buy the biggest, juiciest, reddest apple I can find, quietly and reverently eat it (core and all), then text Allison, "Today I'm remembering Bill."

I hope we can enjoy all the holidays and vacations we do get. But I also hope that we can find the deeper meaning in those days. While you're taking time off for yourself, also take some time to celebrate other people and what they have done for you. It truly is the very least you can do.

FROM MOM: Too often, your dad and I have heard people say things like "We had planned to travel when we retired, but…" or "We always meant to do this together, but…"

Sometimes it's a person who lost their spouse just as they were about to start "enjoying life." Sometimes it's a regretful parent who let the days slip away into decades until they no longer had a relationship with their grown kids.

That's why we've been so adamant about carrying out our family traditions—and encouraging you to do the same. Life is happening now, so just do it! If you have a unique idea, something special in mind, go for it! Do not put off living life until it's too late.

One time, bless his heart, your dad wanted to be romantic, so he bought a kiddie pool and set it up in the middle of our bedroom. This was in the attic apartment we lived in for seven years; it had no heat and no air conditioning, so it was uncomfortable 24/7. Dad heated up water in a kettle and kept running from the kitchen to the (second-story) bedroom to fill the pool with boiling water.

Finally, after about an hour, we had a "hot tub"—but the water was so hot, it almost scalded me! Dad added some bathwater to the mix but ended up cooling the water too much, leaving us sitting in room-temperature water in an unstable plastic pool in our bedroom. On top of everything, he had given zero thought to how we were going to empty the pool once we were done.

It took your dad five hours to throw together what was ultimately a terrible hot tub experience. But I *love* that he tried. I hope you kids don't stop trying, either!

Cook the quirky dinner. Drive the ridiculous route. Camp in the living room. Let your life be full of stories you're glad to tell, not just regrets about the things you meant to do.

TRADITIONS CHECKLIST

- Are there traditions that are unique to your family?

- Do you try to come up with new ideas for common holidays?

- Do you want to create some new experiences?

- Do not allow another family to make you feel inferior just because you do things differently.

- Be willing to fail.

did not of

leaving you which you mu...

d & do, have, you mu...

my real feeling of this mo...

my ... commence

...ds you my ... approache...

to offer. Caroline I am ...

...ears from perceived not su...

that I have nervous are ...

moment I love ...

Caroline My dearest Car...

tears ...

VALUES

The Value of Purpose

The Value of Respect

The Value of Diligence

The Value of Self-Discipline

The Value of Humility

The Value of Being a Lifetime Learner

The Value of Generosity

The Value of Marriage

The Value of Faith

The Value of Righteousness

The Value of Words

The Value of Love

The Value of Thinking for Yourself

The Value of Traditions

The Value of Hospitality

The Value of Purity

Chapter 18

MOM GIGGLES WHEN SHE GETS NERVOUS

"Service to many leads to greatness."

—Jim Rohn

THE VALUE OF HOSPITALITY

There will be times in your life when you simply do something stupid.

Your mom is a master hostess. She oozes hospitality and often seeks opportunities to express that gift. She really is quite amazing. It's because of her hospitality that this incident took place. Some people are "nice." Some people are "friendly." Your mom is those things, too, but when she plays host, she's so much more. She anticipates people's needs before they speak, and somehow she makes even the most awkward spaces feel warm and welcome.

I'm not nearly as hospitable as she is, nor do I long for an endless stream of dinner guests. But being married to her pretty much guarantees that we will, indeed, never stop entertaining. And I have learned, often through trial, error, and disaster, that there's value in stretching yourself to welcome others, even when it doesn't come naturally.

When we got married, the only place we could afford was an apartment located in the attic of an abandoned house. Yes, you read that right. The owners of the house had passed away about a decade before, and the son who inherited the house did nothing to clean out his parents' stuff, even leaving the canned food in the kitchen. However, he did rent out the attic, which had a separate entrance.

This apartment was equipped with ... well, nothing. No heat. No air. No insulation. No ceiling fans. We did have carpet in the (minuscule) bathroom, but the kitchen was so small, the refrigerator and the stove couldn't be opened at the same time. The entire apartment was approximately 500 square feet. In all honesty, looking back on it now, the apartment is just as miserable as it was then. Inside, it was *always* hotter in summer and colder in winter than it was outside. It was also stuffy, and we always had some type of mold growing in from the rest of the house underneath us.

It was truly one of the most inhospitable places to live, let alone to invite guests into. But that didn't stop your mom. Every week or so, we would have someone over for dinner. She never waited for perfect conditions; she just made do with what we had. She made people feel like they belonged. It was never about impressing; it was about connecting.

In the spring of 1995, we invited a newlywed couple over to have dinner with us. Mom made Mexican chicken with green beans. After dinner, she cleaned up while I entertained our guests.

This sweet couple sat down on our new futon. It was our first purchase on credit. The futon sat in the middle of the tiny room, taking up half the space. There was only a little room around it to stand or walk toward the door.

The wife of this couple was petite—and I mean *really* petite, like a life-size doll. She sat down on that futon and immediately twisted her legs into a tight cross-legged knot.

Meanwhile, I stood in front of the couple, awkwardly trying to make small talk. Just then, our dog came into the room and started playing in the space behind the futon.

I looked down, and there at my feet was one of her chew toys: a tough rubber ball made for dogs who chew aggressively. Suddenly, as if possessed by the spirit of a pro baseball player, I felt an overwhelming urge to pick up the ball and pitch it to my dog.

Like an outfielder scooping up a line drive hit to center field, I adjusted my stance, stepped forward, and threw that ball with *everything I had*.

The moment the toy left my hand, I knew the angle was off. My brain, only just catching up with my body, was yelling, *No, abort! Abort!* But it was already too late.

Time seemed to slow down. For a split second, I made eye contact with the wife…

…then the ball hit her square between the eyes!

The poor woman yelped and folded up like a suitcase, her head falling into her lap. I still wince whenever I remember the sound of that rubber toy hitting her face. But that sound was quickly replaced by a worse one: deep, guttural crying. Not a sniffle or a polite whimper, but the kind of sobbing that stops everything in its tracks. And it was all my fault.

Of course, our guest's crying and my rapid-fire pleas of "I'm so, so sorry!" were not the only sounds that filled the room then.

Mom had finished the dishes and stepped out of the kitchen just in time to witness everything. Anyone who knows her can tell you she laughs nervously when things are not going well, so that nervous laugh was also added to the mix. No joke, it was the single most embarrassing moment of my entire life.

I looked at her husband, who was staring off into space and lightly rubbing his wife's back. Neither of us wanted to make eye contact. What could he even do? Defend her? Comfort her? Carry her out? Some situations just don't have a script. This was one of them.

After a grueling twenty minutes of crying, apologizing, nervous giggling, and dry heaving, the husband simply picked his "closed suitcase" wife up by the handle and they went home. Your mom and I didn't even speak of the incident that night. We just laid down in the humid, stagnant shame that we knew we deserved.

PARENTS: TEACH YOUR CHILDREN MANNERS

About ten days after "the incident," we received a note in the mail. The return address was that of the couple we had invited over. We opened the note with apprehension, but much to our surprise, it turned out to be a thank-you note:

Lee and JoAnne, thank you so much for having us over for dinner last week. The Mexican chicken and green beans were very tasty. We appreciate you thinking of us.

P.S. We had a ball!

It was the most gracious, generous, and perfectly timed note we've ever received. That postscript was pure comedic genius. They could have ignored us. They could have never spoken to us again. Instead, they responded with kindness and humor. We haven't forgotten it since.

This experience taught us a valuable lesson about hospitality: The worst, most humiliating things can happen, and it will still turn out okay in the end. Opening your home to others definitely has its risks, but showing others that you care about them is worth it.

We had the most embarrassing thing happen to us in the middle of an attempt to show hospitality. It would have made sense for us to give up trying to host anyone in that apartment ever again. But that is not who your mom is, as I have seen time and time again. Her home exudes warmth. She is a "Proverbs 31" woman who puts herself out there to make others comfortable. Even in the smallest apartment, even after the worst night, she never stopped inviting people in. That's what makes her hospitality a calling and not just a skill.

Sometimes, maybe even most times, putting others first is really hard. "Others" is a pretty broad term. Sometimes it means giving up a parking spot or your seat on a bus. Sometimes it's working at the nursery when no one else can. Sometimes it's helping to set up before or clean up after a party, a bridal shower, or a football party. Sometimes it means picking up someone else's trash. Sometimes it means helping someone move when you don't feel like it.

This self-sacrifice is often seen by the secular world as also self-defeating. But if we believe in a God that loves us, there is something magical that happens when we put others first: Our needs get taken care of, too!

We must create an environment in which people feel comfortable. This is where your mom excels! JoAnne Bailey has a magic about her that creates an environment many have referred to as "warm," "hospitable," and "homey." This is a talent and a gift that you all had the privilege of experiencing as you grew up in our home.

As the husband of a "master hostess," it was hard sometimes to get you all to appreciate this quality. As I was "prepping you," you would often say things like "But Dad, we're having company *again*?" And I would reply, "Yes, and you are going to be nice and respectful. When they ask you questions, you are going to look them in the eye and answer them clearly."

I do believe that one of the reasons you didn't initially appreciate all the company was that we used it as a teaching opportunity. In time, though, you realized that many of these friends we invited over had kids of their own. From then on, you would ask, "Hey, can we invite so-and-so over for dinner on Friday night?"

On top of having new playmates, once you realized that we would always serve your favorite meal (stromboli) when someone new came over, you seemed to be more open to company.

Today, it warms your mom's heart to see how all of you, in your own unique ways, like to host your friends. We have talked so much about how you like to host football games, Bible studies, pool parties, and card games at your homes. We love how much your mom's hospitality has rubbed off on you all. You make us so proud!

Hospitality is born out of a love and respect for others. This is not the most popular idea in a self-centered world, but we have watched it bring all manner of benefits to those who choose to put others first. Stromboli may not be the solution for world peace, but in our home, it certainly made a delicious peace offering!

> *"Do nothing from selfish ambition or conceit, but in humility count others more significant than yourselves. Let each of you look not only to his own interests, but also to the interests of others." (Philippians 2:3–4)*

FROM MOM: Your dad said some nice things about me in this chapter. I don't know about all that, but I do know that it fills my heart with joy to see that people feel comfortable in my home.

Making others feel welcome and like they matter is a skill that's worth honing. Use it well.

HOSPITALITY CHECKLIST

- Do your friends feel welcome in your home?

- Do you think everything needs to be perfect before others can visit your home?

- Are you too busy to invite people over?

- Be willing to put yourself out there for others.

- Your love for others will show through your hospitality.

VALUES

The Value of Purpose

The Value of Respect

The Value of Diligence

The Value of Self-Discipline

The Value of Humility

The Value of Being a Lifetime Learner

The Value of Generosity

The Value of Marriage

The Value of Faith

The Value of Righteousness

The Value of Words

The Value of Love

The Value of Thinking for Yourself

The Value of Traditions

The Value of Hospitality

The Value of Purity

Chapter 19

OH! OH! ICE-COLD MILK AND AN OREO COOKIE....

*"I will not let anyone walk through
my mind with their dirty feet."*

— MAHATMA GANDHI

*"An excellent wife who can find? She is far
more precious than jewels. ... Charm is
deceitful, and beauty is vain, but a woman
who fears the Lord is to be praised."*

(PROVERBS 31:10, 30)

THE VALUE OF PURITY

O f all the delicious snacks on the market, none can compare to the greatest cookies ever made: Oreos. Yet I once wrote a sternly worded letter to Nabisco, the company that makes them. Why? To complain that they were diluting the brand.

I had noticed that aside from the regular (perfect) Oreos, Nabisco was making Double Stuf Oreos and Big Stuf Oreos. Later, they would even make Oreos in a variety of odd flavors and themes: springtime, red velvet, peanut butter, lemon, you name it.

My problem was not with their creativity, not at all! It was the fact that Nabisco was spreading the Oreo name too thin. When you think of an Oreo cookie, you picture two black cookies around a white cream center. So if you substitute the white filling with red velvet, what exactly does the word "Oreo" even mean anymore? The name lost its weight. The cookie's identity was blurred. That black-and-white simplicity, the very thing that made Oreos iconic, was suddenly optional. And to me, that meant the brand wasn't being protected.

The straw that broke the camel's back was when they came out with an "Uh-Oh Oreo." The advertising made it seem like they got the production lines crossed and accidentally made the cookies vanilla and the filling chocolate.

So, I wrote a letter advocating for a change—not that Nabisco stop making new varieties, just that they stop calling all of them "Oreos." I argued that only black cookies with white cream should be Oreos, as that was the purest definition of the word. All the other varieties could still be associated with the brand—for example, "Peanut Butter Cookie, made by the creators of Oreo"—without having the same name. In fact, I felt so strongly about this that I even referred to the other cookie flavors as "an abomination"!

I know this sounds silly, but I really did write that letter. I received no response from Nabisco, but my point here is this: You have something very special with an Oreo. You should protect it. You should guard it. You should respect it in its purest form. You shouldn't let just any sandwich cookie masquerade as an Oreo. There are cheap imitations, but none of them are the real thing.

The same is true of purity. It's something deeply valuable, not because it's rare or old-fashioned, but because it was designed with a specific purpose in mind. Letting culture redefine it, repackage it, and treat it like just another "cookie" distorts its meaning.

This short chapter on the subject of purity was a last-minute addition to this book. While we were writing it, our pastor, Scott Parkison, was preaching a series of sermons on the subject of purity, which drew a lot of attention and questions. As we considered the subject of purity from a biblical perspective, we felt we should include a chapter on this important and sensitive subject.

Your virginity is special. Protect it. Guard it. Don't let someone convince you to flippantly give away your innocence. This isn't just biblical advice (although I believe the Bible is all we need); multiple studies on this subject have come to the same conclusion: Couples who wait until marriage to be intimate are far happier than those who don't. The longer we've lived, the more we've seen this play out in real life.

Even "outercourse" is a cheap substitute for abstinence until marriage. I know this is an uncomfortable subject, especially coming from your mom and dad, but trust us when we say this one choice can be the difference between a good marriage and a great marriage.

Premarital sex can lead to a lot of pain and regret, and our deepest, most heartfelt wish is that you'll all be spared from that. We understand that this is not culturally "in vogue," but then again, much of this book is about swimming against the current.

Purity won't win you applause. If anything, it will make you feel like the odd one out. But it will guard your heart. And your heart is worth guarding.

Boys, you must put on the brakes in these situations. That will be your saving grace. Please believe us: Real strength isn't charging forward. It's knowing when to stop, when to walk away, when to be the kind of man who values his future more than his feelings.

We beg you, for your own good, do not cave in to momentary temptation. It is never worth it.

It never feels like a big deal until it's too late. And then it's the only thing you wish you could take back.

Once, I had planned to spend some "alone time" with my high school girlfriend. My dad had some incredibly wise words for me. He explained that the Bible is full of calls to rise, stand tall, and face the challenges of this life head on with the help of the Holy Spirit. Ephesians 6 even compares this to putting on armor in preparation for spiritual battle. This type of fighting language is woven throughout Scripture.

There is one exception to this, however, and that's in the subject of purity. The Bible, in its inspired wisdom, all but yells at you to *flee* all types of sexual temptation until you are married. God knows that when you are in the middle of *that* moment, you may not be able to withstand the temptation. So instead of trying to be strong, we need to avoid situations where that temptation might arise in the first place.

That's not weakness; that's wisdom. God isn't setting limits to restrict us. He's laying down boundaries to protect us.

You don't have to take it from us, though. Look around. Plenty of people who succumbed to that momentary lapse in judgment would tell you it wasn't worth it. Talk to the couples who have been married for twenty, thirty, or forty years and who have only been with each other. Then, look to the Bible for guidance.

Let these stories help guide your choices. Not the movies. Not the internet. Real people. Real marriages. Real consequences.

Please, guard yourself. Your future spouse will appreciate it.

PURITY CHECKLIST

- Are you lax in your efforts to protect your kids from their own curiosity?
- Do you allow your teenager too much time alone with their boyfriend/girlfriend?
- Are you protecting yourself from drifting?
- Flee all forms of sexual temptation.
- Love your spouse with white-hot intensity.

Chapter 20

MORE TO COME

As we reflect on this labor of love, we are struck by our huge inadequacies. We see you falter in one area or another, and we know that, at least in part, it's because we personally failed in that same area. While we want to live out a life that exemplifies all the values in this book, we know we don't. That gap between what we wanted to model and what we actually did humbles us. It also reminds us why we wanted to write this all down. These values weren't just habits we hoped you'd pick up. They were virtues we deeply believed in, even when we struggled to live them consistently.

We also know that you love us and do not want to disappoint us. We are aware of the pressure we sometimes put on you with our expectations, whether we speak them aloud or not. There's a weight that comes with being deeply known and deeply loved. We hope you never feel like you have to earn our approval. We love you fully, in all your messy human glory.

When your mom and I are gone, we hope this work will help you fill in the gaps of our parenting. Everything we wanted to be as parents is in this book, even if we didn't always live up to that ideal.

We are praying for you. We love you. We want you to have a better relationship with Jesus than we do, and we want you to have more success than we had. We want you to have awesome spouses, great kids, and impactful careers.

We want you to live boldly, love deeply, and pursue purpose without fear. But even if none of those boxes are checked, we hope you know this: You are already enough.

We know you want these things, too. Take heart in knowing that it doesn't matter what you do, only who you are. One of our greatest assignments from God was to raise you. And that assignment was our joy. You have been our life's greatest calling, and we have never taken that lightly.

Your mom and I were once invited to a barbecue to celebrate our friends' twenty-five-year-old daughter's new job. She would be moving to downtown Chicago the very next morning. As we all gathered around for a toast, her father said, "When you raise your kids to be bold and brave, it shouldn't surprise you when they make bold and brave decisions."

It sounds so logical, but that doesn't mean it's easy. Letting go never is, especially when you've spent decades pouring your whole soul into someone else's becoming.

Right as our friend was, it's still hard to accept when it comes to your own kids. That same week, Max, then twenty-three, would be marking his first anniversary of relocating to another state, purchasing a house, and starting a new job, all in an effort to further his own budding career.

Meanwhile, Levi, then twenty, was pursuing a new entrepreneurial endeavor: starting his own line dancing business. He had been teaching himself all the line dancing songs and moves and had even been asked by numerous groups to lead a dance party, so he saw an opportunity to make money from his new hobby.

We were also making final preparations to drive Emma, then eighteen, to college two hours away. She'd earned an athletic scholarship, and that week, she would be moving into the dorm and getting acquainted with her new team.

And finally, still that same week, Audrey would be turning sixteen. We had already found a car for her, which she purchased herself with the money she'd saved from working over the summer at Chick-fil-A.

All of you kids, each in your own way, were making bold and brave decisions.

> *"Leadership is the awesome responsibility to see those around us rise." —Simon Sinek*

Parenting *is* leadership. You must set out to send out, and then *expect* your kids to go. You will cry, but you will bounce back.

You will make it. Because you will have been intentional from the beginning. You will be a deliberate parent. Go be a proud one, too.

All that said, there are some failures that we need to acknowledge. Of all the things we worked to teach and correct you on, there are just some things you simply did not get while living in our house:

- How to open a box of cereal
- How to mow the grass
- How to walk softly
- How to clear the table after dinner
- How to take the trash out
- How to open mail
- How to write a check
- How to turn off lights before leaving a room
- How to close the basement door
- How to put appointments in your calendar
- How to screw on the lid of the peanut butter jar
- How to replace the toilet paper roll
- How to peel a banana without mushing the end

Of course, this is a joke, not an actual list of shortcomings. None of us are perfect or good at things right away. In fact, it might take you decades to fully embrace some of the lessons we taught you. That's okay. We believe we did our best to place those values on the shelves of your hearts for you to draw from in the future. And we trust that when the time comes, you'll remember. Even if you don't remember the lectures or the lists or the late-night talks, you'll remember what matters.

If you have young kids, there is one book I recommend to help you to raise them with the right motivation: *Shepherding a Child's Heart* by Tedd Tripp. It's by far the best book I have personally read that helps parents get to the heart of why we parent and gives us motivation to keep going when it gets tough.

Kids, we pray that we have decades left with you, but we didn't want to wait to write this book for you.

We didn't want to let the good intentions behind our parenting slip away. We wanted you to have our words while we're still around to speak them.

For those of you outside of our family reading this, we encourage you to start your own traditions, delineate your own values, create your own habits, and do things with purpose.

We are cheering for you. Good, faithful, intentional, deliberate, sacrificial parents are not common. Too often, people get caught up in the many challenges of life, and while they mean to teach respect, they never do. They intend to encourage hard work, but in the end, they wind up doing all the work for their kids. Parents mean well but don't model their values as often as they would like. And yet, those who keep showing up, even imperfectly, can still change the trajectory of a generation.

Do you know how we know that? Because that describes us. In full, no-makeup transparency, we failed more than we succeeded. We know that. But we kept on trying.

> *"For the righteous falls seven times and rises again, but the wicked stumble in times of calamity." (Proverbs 24:16)*

Here are a few final pieces of advice:

Do *not* feel like you have to homeschool to accomplish everything you want to as parents. Homeschooling has its benefits, but it also has its drawbacks. Do what's right for your family, zero judgment from us.

Consistency is *way* more important than complexity. You can have a three-dimensional, glow-in-the-dark, holographic chore chart, but if you aren't willing to make sure all those chores are done every day, your kids will not see its worth. One simple chore per day, every day, is enough to instill good values.

If you allow your kid to quit an activity they begged you to let them do, whether it's a sport, an instrument, or a play, then you are teaching them the opposite of hard work. Make them finish the season, semester, or rehearsal schedule. They may be miserable, but they won't forget it.

Dig deep to find your own set of values. Don't put this off. We *all* operate from a set of values, either ones we chose ourselves or ones that were chosen for us. Without a solid foundation of values to work from, your kids will receive mixed messages. You can't insist they say "Yes, sir," and "Yes, ma'am," one month and laugh when they sass you the next, or else they will learn that respect is circumstantial. Permitting is promoting. Define your values, then make daily choices that reflect them.

When you think about what you might leave behind for your kids and grandkids, consider the idea of legacy. What did you do to stop a generational stronghold? Did you beat an addiction and allow God to use you in a volunteer ministry? Did you change jobs so you can be at more of your son's baseball games? Did you go from being someone who didn't care about spiritual matters to being the spiritual leader of your home? Did you love your spouse in front of your kids and show them what a loving marriage looks like? Did you teach them honesty by actually giving back the extra change the cashier gave you by mistake? Did you overcome adversity with humility and speak openly about your faith? Legacy isn't what's written in your obituary. It's what lives on in the people who knew you when you were alive.

Parents, our kids do not so much remember what we say as they remember what we do.

Set the following reminder on your phone to pop up once a day or once a week:

> *My kids are watching me. What do I want them to see?*

Then go live out the answer.

ACKNOWLEDGMENTS

We would like to thank all the friends and family members who poured into us as we grew and who helped establish the values we hold dear.

We are incredibly grateful for the wonderful people of Dotson Memorial, Oak View, Brainard, Laurel Bank, Morristown, Eden Westside, East Maryville, and Stevens Street. We simply do not have the words.

A special thank-you to Dustin Rawls, one of our beta readers, who gave us some incredible feedback that helped make this book better. Dustin, thank you, my friend! ***hugs***

Thank you to Ashley Michael, another of our beta readers, who encouraged us to expand upon our homeschool routine, describe our living room setup, and include more of JoAnne's words. We are so grateful for your helpful comments!

Thank you to Wren Michael, who helped us with some very creative cover designs.

Finally, we want to thank Natalie Beach, who spent so much time advising us on structure, content, grammar, and volume. She also encouraged us to share our personal testimonies, which would have been a huge oversight on our part. There is no way this book would have been as complete and thorough without you, Natalie!